Give a Listen

NCTE Committee on Storytelling

R. Craig Roney, Chair
Wayne State University

Pauletta B. Bracy, Associate Chair
North Carolina Central University

Akua Duku Anokye
Queensborough Community College

John D. Beach
State University of New York–Cortland

Brian J. Conroy
K. R. Smith Elementary, San Jose, California

Sheila Dailey
Mt. Pleasant, Michigan

Brad T. Kerwin
Punahou School, Honolulu, Hawaii

Barbara LeCroy
University of Southern Mississippi

Barbara Lipke
Newton Center, Massachusetts

Alice Phoebe Naylor
Appalachian State University

Tina Ruiz
Rutgers University

Marni Schwartz
The Story Studio, Delmar, New York

Jay C. Stailey
George Washington Carver Elementary School, Baytown, Texas

Ann M. Trousdale
Louisiana State University

Linda Wason-Ellam
University of Saskatchewan

Sue A. Woestehoff
University of Michigan–Flint

Stephanie M. Gerjovich Wright
Delaware Teacher Center, Newark

Barbara Flores, Executive Committee Liaison
California State University

Karen Smith, NCTE Staff Liaison

Give a Listen

Stories of Storytelling in School

Edited by

Ann M. Trousdale
Louisiana State University

Sue A. Woestehoff
University of Michigan–Flint

Marni Schwartz
The Story Studio

National Council of Teachers of English
1111 W. Kenyon Road, Urbana, Illinois 61801-1096

Staff Editors: Sheila A. Ryan and David Hamburg

Cover Design: Loren Kirkwood

Interior Book Design: Doug Burnett

NCTE Stock Number 18461-3050

Library of Congress Cataloging-in-Publication Data

Give a listen : stories of storytelling in school / edited by Ann M.
   Trousdale, Sue A. Woestehoff, Marni Schwartz.
         p. cm.
      Includes bibliographical references.
      ISBN 0-8141-1846-1
      1. Storytelling. I. Trousdale, Ann M. II. Woestehoff, Sue A.
   III. Schwartz, Marni. IV. National Council of Teachers of English.
   LB1042.G53 1994
   372.64'2—dc20   94-12485
                                                        CIP

Contents

Acknowledgments

We would like to express our appreciation to Jennifer Falls, Mary Stokes, Lois Stewart, and Joyce Stevenson for their assistance in the preparation of the manuscript. Special thanks to Stephanie Gerjovich-Wright for her extensive work in selecting and reviewing manuscripts during the initial stages of the development of *Give a Listen*. We also thank the contributors to the book and the members of the NCTE Committee on Storytelling for their contributions to the section on Resources for Storytellers.

Introduction

Storytelling. It's everywhere. Whether you fly on airplanes, take buses, sit in a crowded doctor's office, stand in a line at the grocery store, take a break at the water cooler, or sit with a child or an elder at a family dinner, give a listen. You'll hear stories. Realistic and fantastic. Stories learned in the living. Stories honed by countless tellings. Chances are you'll find yourself passing one on. We are a storying people. We make sense of our lives through stories; we understand our histories and glimpse our futures through stories—our own and the stories of others.

Today in the teaching of the language arts we are breaking new ground as we build classroom communities in which readers and writers engage with language in personally significant ways. We look for means of making our classrooms learning environments in which language is used for authentic purposes—to explain, to persuade, to entertain, to report, to teach, to discover. We've turned to children's early oral language acquisition in order to reevaluate our approach to literacy development. It is time we looked more closely at storytelling as an important and revitalizing component of our classroom environments.

In elementary classrooms, teachers are seeing that young children still find delight in the retelling of favorite tales, learning the rhythms of language beginning with patterns and repetitions as simple as "Trip-trap, trip-trap, trip-trap." Can older students learn more sophisticated language patterns through the telling of stories as well? We believe they can—and do. For older children, the oral sharing of stories breaks down walls of isolation, often becoming the glue that holds together a diverse set of community members, giving them a common language experience along with a deeper understanding of one another. Personal narratives and original fiction composed orally before a receptive audience often develop into lively pieces of writing; or they may simply exist in a classroom's own oral tradition. Readers and writers find new meaning in stories that they have read or composed by stepping into them dramatically through storytelling. Oral storytelling also becomes a route to understanding other cultures and worlds of long ago or far away. As we look with new eyes at reading and writing, we must look as well at storytelling.

Throughout the United States, storytelling is experiencing a revival. What started as a small group of tellers coming together in Jonesborough, Tennessee, twenty years ago to share their love of the oral tale is now a huge festival at which tens of thousands of people gather in tents scattered over the town. Why? Simply because we are able to see ourselves and our world reflected in the images conveyed by the storyteller. Perhaps we are lifted up by glimpsing a more ideal self or a less complicated world. Perhaps we recognize a familiar antagonist and come to understand the nature of our own struggles more clearly. Perhaps we are looking for the touch of humor which will enable us to take ourselves and our own lives less seriously. Perhaps we need the hope which comes from the happy ending which many oral tales offer.

The National Council of Teachers of English recognized the need to get teachers talking about the importance of storytelling as an aspect of the language arts program by forming its Committee on Storytelling, which first met at the seventy-fifth annual convention in Philadelphia in 1985. Since then it has worked through convention programs and a recently published NCTE position statement to spread the word about the power of storytelling for the classroom.

This collection grew out of the committee's desire to lure teachers into the world of storytelling. Our committee, made up of a variety of classroom teachers, librarians, university professors, and a few full-time storytellers, recognized a need for a book on storytelling. We began by drafting a traditional textbook, describing the history of storytelling, making lists of reasons storytelling would enhance the curriculum, pulling together objectives and activities galore. However, in the end our compilation seemed disjointed and dry, another uninviting teacher's manual. It lacked the life we knew storytelling possessed.

"We need to tell our stories!" one of our members suggested near the end of a particularly frustrating meeting. Suddenly faces lit up. Yes. Tell our stories. We had all seen storytelling live and breathe in our teaching, in our townships, in our travels. We had each experienced the thrill of trying on a story for the first time and feeling its power over an audience. We had witnessed groups of kids, too, sharing their triumphs and faux pas through personal stories or finding in ancient or familiar tales reverberations of their own lives.

Yes, stories would do it. A call for manuscripts brought forth stories of storytelling from across the country, even a few from across the globe. The many manuscripts that we received confirmed our belief that storytelling is alive and well in classrooms for all ages. We set to work on this collection, knowing that the objectives and lists and activities from our lifeless textbook had been given life through these stories.

Give a Listen is a collection of stories about storytelling. It is not a how-to book about storytelling, though as you read the stories you will find teachers and students describing the processes through which they have discovered—or tapped into—the power of storytelling.

Nor is the book an attempt to formulate theory about storytelling. We have come to see that theory is implicit in the stories one tells; no doubt the theories that undergird these stories will seep through in the telling. But as much as possible, we have attempted to tell our stories without falling into the temptation of stepping aside to explain them. As storytellers, it is our experience that a good story, well told, stands on its own. For those who wish to explore narrative theory more deeply, we have included an annotated list of Resources for Storytellers for such study. Also included in the resources section are annotated bibliographies of books and articles about the art of storytelling, about how to bring storytelling into the classroom, and of favorite collections of stories. Whether you are a beginning storyteller or a teacher who would like to develop your skills and repertoire further, you'll find this list of resources a useful appendix to the book.

As the first collection of its kind, *Give a Listen* describes many of the ways storytelling has been woven into the fabric of the classroom. You'll hear stories about the power of the oral tale to mesmerize listeners; stories about how storytelling has brought shy or reluctant learners into the classroom community; stories about how storytelling became the means of enlivening other areas of the curriculum. You'll hear of tellers who found layers of new meaning in already familiar stories through telling them to a live audience, of writers who gained a new perspective on their compositions through oral redrafting. You'll hear teachers describe how they have come to know students and other faculty members differently through tales told both formally and informally.

All of the stories speak to the classroom teacher, but they also speak to anyone who has shared or who wants to share a good story with an audience. The characters in our stories are preschoolers through adults; the classrooms span the years from elementary school through college. Despite this range, readers will find that within most of the stories are perspectives and experiences that can be applied to learners of all ages.

The collection is divided into three sections. The first section recounts how storytellers get started. It should encourage new tellers, support seasoned ones, and give practical tips for teachers and learners. The stories in the second section tell how teachers have connected storytelling to the teaching of traditional school subjects. We also learn what tellers and listeners come to find out about themselves and others through the stories that are told. The final section tells how storytelling can serve to define and build communities of listeners and learners.

Because natural storytelling exists in the innumerable settings of our lives, more and more teachers are making a place for it in the classroom. Whether you are one of those teachers or one curious to explore ways to set storytelling in motion, you'll discover both the hows and the whys of it here. Give a listen.

I In the Beginning: How Storytellers Get Started

All storytellers have beginnings. This section tells the stories of such beginnings from those of the young preschool child to the seasoned college professor. You will read accounts of individuals whose roots are steeped in the oral tradition and of others for whom oral storytelling seems alien or frightening. You will discover techniques that might nudge you or your students into storytelling or that could assist you in a journey that has already begun.

Jeanne Smith from Oglala Lakota College tells how she reluctantly invited a professional storyteller, Anne Bodman, into her world literature class, then watched in amazement as Bodman cast a spell over her audience. Jeanne soon realized the connection between Bodman's tale and the stories she had heard for years from Calvin Jumping Bull, a longtime Lakota friend and colleague. Jeanne then tells us how she became a storyteller herself and how storytelling became an integral part of her teaching.

Storytelling beginnings are often surprising and unpredictable. Karen Durand tells how natural exchanges occurring during a class walking exercise led into informal storytelling, easily and unselfconsciously enjoyed by all the children. Fresh and original possibilities for storytelling were incorporated as they presented themselves—and the class became a class of "strolling storytellers."

Kerry Mallan's conviction that teachers should listen to their students was a motivating factor in her storytelling work with school children in Australia. Through her accounts of Dwayne and his classmates, we see how these children developed as storytellers, and we learn about a variety of techniques that Kerry used to assist her aspiring young tellers.

Ann Trousdale's family tradition of storytelling led her into sharing personal stories, and then folktales, with three-year-old Tim. Soon Tim was participating in telling the familiar stories, and from there to helping to develop new stories along with Ann. We learn how these experiences with

Tim led her to working out methods of using interactive storytelling in the elementary classroom.

School success is the focus of Marni Schwartz's piece about Sally, a young middle school student, who found confidence in the familiar Br'er Rabbit tales. Sally's development as a storyteller was both enhanced and chronicled by the use of a learning log in which she "talked" about how she worked through the process of becoming a storyteller.

Joe Yukish traces his storytelling roots to his second-generation Slovak-Croatian family and his upbringing in Appalachia. He tells the tale of his coming to have faith in his ability to tell stories, from his first nervous try during a college course to a somewhat more confident telling for his colleagues at a faculty Christmas party. Joe's reflections should encourage us all to tap our own storytelling roots.

We hope that these narratives will inspire and challenge you to become a storyteller yourself or to encourage others in their storytelling ventures. Perhaps they will stimulate you to recall your own storytelling beginnings. Give a listen!

1 The Story's the Thing

Jeanne Smith

I just didn't want a storyteller to come to my class. "You've got to use her, Jeanne. She's a real pro!" My office mate, Dorothy Mack, was trying to convince me to have a storyteller named Anne Bodman tell stories to my world literature class.

"I don't know," I said slowly. "We have so much to cover in that class. I just don't see where I can find the time."

"But Jeanne," Dorothy said, "she does *Tristan and Isolde.*"

"Oh, that's nice." *Tristan and Isolde.* I was too embarrassed to tell Dorothy that I had absolutely no idea what *Tristan and Isolde* was. I couldn't even spell Isolde.

"Oh, Jeanne, you just have to find the time. Anne came to my children's literature class, and the students *loved* her. She did *The Odyssey* and kept them spellbound for a full hour."

Anne's name and phone number, written on a scrap of paper, ended up on my mounting stack of "things to do." This action practically guaranteed that the storytelling idea would be lost forever.

Dorothy and I had been office mates for five years, and friends for several years before that. We both taught composition and literature at Oglala Lakota College, a Native American college chartered by the Oglala Sioux Tribe. The college, in a setting made famous in *Dances with Wolves,* is located on the Pine Ridge Reservation in South Dakota. I trusted Dorothy's opinion and knew that introducing storytelling into my literature course was a good idea. Yet I had apprehensions about inviting a storyteller I didn't know personally.

"Maybe," I thought, "I can get Calvin to tell stories!"

Calvin Jumping Bull has been a friend for more than twenty years. We are both on the faculty of Oglala Lakota College, but our association goes back before the foundation of the college to the late sixties and early seventies, to the heady, youthful days of the War on Poverty. In those days my husband and I worked with VISTA volunteers on the reservation, and we worked with Calvin on a Labor Department program called New Careers. In fact, it was because of the New Careers program that I first heard Calvin tell stories.

Calvin is a lean, wiry Lakota man, seemingly a confirmed bachelor, who has a twinkle in his eye and a story for every occasion. He used to visit us on summer evenings, sitting at our kitchen table for hours telling stories, stories, stories. Although Calvin usually arrived with some problem from the New Careers program to discuss, the real purpose of his visits was the stories and jokes we shared. Also, he understood that my husband and I were in dire need of the subtle cultural education his stories could bring. On many breezy summer evenings when the supper dishes had long been cleared, fresh coffee all consumed, Calvin would be fresh and lively, ready to tell stories late into the night. Calvin must know a thousand stories.

One summer night at our kitchen table, I learned Calvin was illustrating several Iktomi stories, and then using his drawings to tell young children these trickster tales. And so, back in the autumn of 1971, I had invited Calvin to tell these stories to several of my classes. But until Dorothy talked to me about using a storyteller in my classroom in 1987, I hadn't really thought about inviting Calvin back to my class. "Why not!" I thought. "I know him, and he knows me. That seems much better than bringing in someone I don't even know."

Unfortunately, I had been so certain that Calvin *would* be able to come that I had already told my students a storyteller would be part of the semester's experience. But when Calvin and I tried to find a time for him to come to my class, I was chagrined to learn that he was teaching a class about fifty miles away when I had world literature. There was no way he could be my guest storyteller.

I had postponed my call to Anne as long as I dared. My class had already read *Antigone* and *Oedipus Rex* and we were just finishing Achebe's *Things Fall Apart*. After I dialed Anne's number, I muttered to myself, "Well, we passed the best time for *The Odyssey*. At least I know what *The Odyssey* is. What in the world is *Tristan and Isolde*? And even more importantly, why didn't I look it up before making this phone call?"

A friendly voice greeted me, a voice full of laughter. I began to relax. "You've got to use her, Jeanne. She's a pro." Dorothy's words hummed in the back of my mind. Maybe this wouldn't be so bad after all.

I learned many things from my phone conversation with Anne. I learned that she knew many stories, not just *The Odyssey* and *Tristan and Isolde*. I also learned that *Tristan* was probably a very good story to use when my students read *Romeo and Juliet*, partly as a vehicle to discuss the troubadours, romance, and chivalry, and partly just to tune them into the qualities of a tragic romance. I also learned that Anne wasn't at all concerned that I had never heard of *Tristan and Isolde.* I was beginning to look forward to her visit.

By the time Anne arrived to tell *Tristan,* I was a nervous wreck. Several of my strongest students were absent, and the students present were all young mothers with small children in tow. Two things had conspired to create this atypical audience: babysitter problems and the idea that the children might enjoy the story. But I was skeptical. "A two-year-old will never sit still for an hourlong medieval romance," I thought. "This is going to be a disaster!" Anne may have been concerned as well, but she arrived all smiles and seemed quite at ease. I relaxed as best I could, and Anne began.

Before the actual story, Anne gave the class some background information. My eyes drifted to the children. They were already squirming and fussing a little. "They'll never make it," I thought. "How will she handle people getting up in the middle of the story to take their children out? What if some of these toddlers start crawling around, pulling things off shelves, knocking things over?" My stomach was in a tight knot.

Then Anne began her tale: "Once, long ago, when King Arthur was reigning in Britain and King Mark was reigning in Cornwall. . . ." And a magical thing happened. The moment Anne shifted into her "storytelling voice," the children grew absolutely still. I had never seen anything quite like it. During her introduction, Anne's voice didn't hold the children at all. But the storyteller's voice drew all of us in. As the children relaxed and stilled, so did their mothers. And so did I. One very young child fell asleep. But everyone else in the room was held in the spell of this ancient romance for a solid hour, an hour when neither child nor parent squirmed in discomfort. But the moment the storytelling voice stopped, the spell ended. One child whimpered that he needed a drink; another had to get down from her mother's lap and walk around the room, talking and shuffling papers around the table. The question-answer session wasn't working, and we all took a break.

I will never forget the spell I saw created that day. I envied it terribly. "What must it be like," I thought, "to create that kind of magic?" Shakespeare's "The play's the thing" transformed in my mind to: "The story's the thing." It was the story, and the expert telling of the story, that held my students and their young children. I hadn't realized that story had such power, even after teaching literature for many years! And although I had been under the spell of Calvin's stories, and the stories of several other Lakota people, I hadn't made the emotional connection between the Lakota oral tradition and the oral tradition of the Greeks and of Europeans. It wasn't until experiencing the oral telling of stories from my own cultural tradition that I fully understood the power that the Lakota oral tradition had for my students.

During the summer of 1990 Calvin, Anne, and I obtained a grant from the South Dakota Committee on the Humanities to run a three-week teacher institute on storytelling. Anne and Calvin were to be storytellers-consultants, and the three of us formed a teaching team. Our goal was to teach a group of South Dakota teachers, many of them from reservation schools, how to tell stories and how to integrate storytelling into their classrooms. My secret hidden agenda, however, was that I wanted to learn how to tell stories myself.

Both Calvin and Anne had been guest storytellers in my classrooms several times since Anne first told *Tristan* to my students and their children. The same magic entered the room each time, although never with the drama of my first encounter. I was still envious of that quiet, focused spell a storyteller could cast. I wanted to do that too.

The first week of the storytelling institute focused upon traditional tales, tales which had originated in an oral tradition. During this week Calvin told a number of Lakota stories, and Anne told stories from around the world. Meanwhile the participants, all elementary and secondary teachers, were each developing a tale, working each day in small groups to polish the tale. Although I was the central administrator of the institute, during the storytelling practice I became a student.

The tale I selected was "The Wife of Bath's Tale" from *The Canterbury Tales.* This was a surprising choice for me, because I had never been drawn to *The Canterbury Tales* in college. Books on Tape changed all that, however! It was while driving through a blinding prairie rainstorm, listening to a tape of *The Canterbury Tales,* that I fell in love with Chaucer, and especially with the gaptoothed Wife of Bath.

In our small groups we worked on all aspects of our story. We drew it, we talked it, and I sang part of mine. As the group work continued, the tale began to sink into my bones and become part of me. I knew exactly how my knight looked, and the young girl he raped became imprinted on my mind. I could see the towns visited by the knight on his yearlong quest for the answer to Guinevere's question: "What is it that women most desire?" And the last scene of the story in the wedding chamber became as clear to me as if I had been there.

Each participant developed one story to tell to the whole group during the final week of the institute. Although I had developed a personal story about my mother-in-law that I liked a great deal, I knew that "The Wife of Bath's Tale" was my favorite. As we sat in a large circle—twenty people who had laughed and cried together for three weeks while working on our stories—no one really wanted to say goodbye. Our stories became our farewell gift to one another. Anne taped the stories, and three weeks ago I slipped the tape into my recorder as I drove to class, and listened again to those wonderful tales.

Then came my own voice singing: "Oh, hard is the fortune of all womankind. . . ." and my tale began. "Long, long ago, in the days of King Arthur, when fairies still lived in England, there lived a handsome, lusty knight." Listening to my own story, the first time I had found the courage to do so, I delighted again in the laughter, the gasps, the general response of my audience. I have told that story several times now, once to teenagers in a youth group, another time to an adult Sunday school class, once to my family around a campfire, to a high school English class on the reservation, and to several world literature classes. It has always been well received. But that first audience reaction, the reaction Anne captured on tape, will always be the most important to me. These fellow beginning storytellers had helped me see, touch, smell, and taste my story. They had lived it with me and seemed to catch every nuance. Their laughter several times alerted me to an irony, a twist, a humorous juxtaposition that I hadn't even seen myself.

Now, I can't imagine my life without storytelling. I am constantly amazed at how good it feels to tell a story, even to the air. I often practice my stories as I drive along in my car or pull weeds in the garden. And I have begun to tell stories to my students as a natural, integrated part of the curriculum. It is probably easiest to integrate and develop stories for the children's literature course I inherited from Dorothy Mack when she retired. After they hear my stories, students often tell their own: modern ghost stories, traditional tales, and stories from their own lives. Because the Lakota culture is rooted in such a strong oral tradition, storytelling comes easily to many of my students. Moreover, because most students in the course plan to be elementary teachers, this is a valuable skill for them to develop.

World literature is the class where I've had the most fun with storytelling, however. I use story to help capture my students and lead them into literary works they sometimes find prohibitive. I try to find stories that create an awe, or an amazement. I'd be delighted if I could get their mouths to drop open! So far I've developed a Norwegian creation story, a Gabriel García Marquéz story, and "The Wife of Bath's Tale," all as introductions to new sections of the course. I've found that these stories quiet and deepen us all and prepare us to explore new realities. The oral story seems to make the literature more accessible and more human, perhaps because most of the literature we study is so directly linked to an oral tradition or to specific stories from that tradition. For example, I have used *Oedipus Rex, Antigone, Iphigenia, Things Fall Apart, Innocent Erendire, Rashamon, The Taming of the Shrew,* and *Ceremony* at various times in the course. All can be linked in one way or another to an oral tradition.

Perhaps the most important aspect of storytelling in the curriculum from my perspective, however, is a personal one. Telling stories makes me happy. There is something therapeutic for me in the process of selecting, developing, and telling a story. Although I have never fully understood why a particular story calls out to be told, I have learned to trust my instincts and learn those stories that call to me. For example, while developing "The Wife of Bath's Tale," I realized I was drawn to the story because the knight's punishment for rape was handled by the women of the court, rather than by King Arthur, who would have put the knight to death. The knight's yearlong search for an understanding of women changed him quite dramatically, at least in my version of the story. And as I struggled to develop this imaginary knight, I wrestled with memories and feelings long forgotten. When the story was finally developed, I was at peace. Yet each time I tell the story again, the peace deepens. With almost every telling I find myself adding a nuance or changing some detail which helps me understand both the story and myself a little better. In fact, a few weeks ago when I first heard myself tell the story on tape, the ending made me cry. It never had that effect on me before. The next day when I told the story in world literature class, I felt the story change again, affected by my tears of the previous day. A bit of the magic I had seen when Anne first told *Tristan* reappeared. No one moved. And by the end of the story one student fought to hold back tears. When the story was over, there was a deep, still silence. Although no one had a question to ask, or an observation to make, I knew the story had hit its mark. "So this is how it feels," I said to myself.

The story's the thing.

2 The Strolling Storytellers

Karen P. Durand

In a teacher's workroom at a school in South Carolina: Here, let me fix you a cup of coffee. I'll have one too as I run off some papers. You must be the sub in the first grade. I hope your day wasn't anything like mine: bus duty, new student, sick child! By two o'clock I was ready to take a walk. Even one mile is a great stress leveler.

Where do I walk, you ask?

Would you believe my whole class is walking to Washington, D.C.! Actually we're doing a wellness program. Each time the class walks a mile on the playground we count a mile for each walker and measure it on a map and graph. So far we have covered 321 miles. We should hit the target 500 miles next month. That's when the high school band comes and we parade the final mile. Actually the walk is to develop fitness and self-esteem. But you know what happened this year? We've become strolling storytellers!

Did you want sugar or cream?

Sure, I'd love to tell you how we got started with the stories. It was accidental, really. I probably couldn't have planned it.

While we walk, small groups form and a few students trek with me. They usually talk about things at home or about friends. You know there really isn't the time or atmosphere for that in the classroom. Objectives have taken over.

So one day Allison told me about her grandfather's tractor. Then I spoke about going to my uncle's farm when I was young. Actually, it was a good story because my brother and I went up to the forbidden hayloft to play and he fell from the mow to the floor below. The ones that were listening begged for another story from my childhood. But I couldn't remember anything as exciting as that on the spot. The diplomat within said, "Let's swap stories. You tell one, I'll tell one." By then there were several in the group and they all had something to share, a "Once I . . ." remembrance.

In class the next day, quite coincidentally, we looked at the elements of a story. After my retelling of "Uncle Fred's Farm," the children identified setting, characters, and plot with a beginning, middle, and end. I invited them to think of a story for the next walk.

We logged some miles again after a particularly chatty day. Several children wanted to tell a story as we looped the field. The first was about a dog that was lost when the family went on vacation. Perhaps I was too generous with enthusiasm for the telling, because the rest of the stories were about dogs, too.

Later a thought struck. The children were telling a genre of story. Are you familiar with the Jack Tales? You know the stories with the boy who doesn't seem bright but always outwits everyone. That's a genre.

That week I went to our library and got several collections of stories. The children saw how tales from the Brothers Grimm were alike in some ways and how the Leo Lionni stories were also similar. Some children then retold their stories from the walk and we named them "The Dog Tails."

Then I suggested that those who wanted to read a story could retell it in their own words on the next walk. With this step, more children became interested. Perhaps the books made them feel like real storytellers. During the week, I helped a few organize the main events in the story they chose. Then for many miles everyone enjoyed hearing literature. Unfortunately I didn't listen to them all; some shared with one or two friends.

More coffee? Let me refill your cup. Don't worry, it's decaf. But who couldn't sleep after a day like today!

What else you ask? Let's see, after telling stories from books, the librarian arranged for a local storyteller to visit. The children were introduced to some of the more technical elements like expression and style. She was good.

As for walking, the jessamine were in bloom. We gathered some flowers and different kinds of leaves for pressing. Spring was the main focus of those first beautiful days.

Then came the mushrooms! You know I've walked around that playground about three hundred times. But Mother Nature always has some surprises! There down by the left-hand corner fence was a stand of tiny mushrooms. They must have sprung up overnight. We all got down on the ground for a closer look. Imagine being small enough to live there, like Stuart Little!

Instead of saying, "Tomorrow we can write about this," I thought of the stories. In campfire style I began a story about the adventure of a little mouse. At a critical point, I stopped and someone else picked up the story. Soon the mouse had brothers, sisters, and a whole village. An unpredictable history twisted and turned as we ambled along.

I could see that each storyteller had made an impression. Each part of the saga was unique. Many were beginning to realize that they could have an impact on an audience, friends on the trail in this case, with their imagination and language.

But that wasn't all. Later in class some children made finger puppets to retell their favorite parts. "A class of giants was walking to Washington. Suddenly the ground began shaking. Our little village was nearly trampled by a Nike the size of a football field."

You can see that storytelling opens new arenas for creativity. Just the mushrooms alone spawned puppets, writing, and art work. And like the mushrooms, all that was spontaneous.

I also noticed that a few shy ones who would never have the courage or inclination to get up in front of the class for an oral presentation felt comfortable spinning their own quiet yarns on the path when the crowd thinned. In class we talked about stories told one-on-one, like a telephone conversation. One talks, the other listens.

Speaking of listening. These kids' skills had to improve! We told stories while walking on the perimeter of soccer games! But I've always thought that storytelling fine tunes our ability to listen and imagine. Don't you agree?

Well, I've about talked your ear off. I know what long days you subs put in too.

What? You're not a sub?

You're from the Smithsonian Institute!

Me? Attend a workshop on storytelling in Washington this summer?

Count me in!

3 "Do It Again, Dwayne": Finding Out about Children as Storytellers

Kerry Mallan

Okay Dwayne, whenever you're ready." I give Dwayne a nod and sit down with the rest of the class on the floor. Dwayne settles on the chair in front of his classmates. He leans forward with his hands joined together. He gives a penetrating look that encompasses everyone.

There's a nervous twitter from a couple of the children, then . . . absolute silence. Dwayne's story is about to begin.

"In the dark, dark woods . . . . there was a dark, dark path."

Dwayne's voice is slow, almost robotic, and the look continues to snare all of his listeners. He continues . . .

"On the dark, dark path, there was a dark, dark house."

Again he pauses and with the skill of a professional storyteller allows enough time for the audience's excitement to bubble slowly to the surface.

"In the dark, dark house, there was a dark . . . . . dark . . . . . staircase."

Another pause. Dwayne leans forward a little. The audience responds instinctively and leans a little closer towards Dwayne. Teller and audience are locked in what would appear to an outsider as a conspiracy of intrigue.

The story continues.

"Up the dark, dark staircase . . . . there was a dark . . . . dark . . . . room."

The audience giggles nervously. Dwayne knows he has hooked his audience, and now he has to reel them in slowly before the magic of his line breaks.

"In the dark, dark room there was a . . . . . . dark, dark cupboard."

A short pause. Dwayne slowly moves his head from one side to the other and makes eye contact with everyone in the room.

"And in the dark, dark cupboard there was a dark, dark shelf."

His voice is now quite soft. The audience is waiting, anticipating, enjoying.

"On the dark, dark shelf . . . there was a dark, dark box."

Some of the children glance at each other, eyes sparkling, acknowledging each other's excitement.

"In the dark, dark box" (Dwayne's voice is very soft and slowly he continues) *"there was . . . . A GHOST!"*

Dwayne almost shouts the last two words and simultaneously leaps from his chair towards his audience.

It works! The audience shrieks with fright. Then there is a spontaneous applause and rightly so, for Dwayne has earned it. Then the talk breaks out. Everyone responds vocally to Dwayne's storytelling.

"That was great, Dwayne."

"Yeah, you really gave us a scare."

"I liked his eyes. They looked like Frankenstein."

"There was a GHOST!"

"I knew you were going to say that."

"I thought it was going to be something scary, like a skeleton."

"Yeah, a skeleton."

"Or Dracula."

"Do it again Dwayne."

"Can I go next?"

This was not the first and only time Dwayne told his classmates a story. Over the next six weeks, Dwayne and the other children continued to tell stories. The stories were rich and varied. Stories about their families, their secret fears, stories that their parents, grandparents, or friends had told them, stories they found in books, school stories, jokes, camp stories, Sunday school stories, stories from last night's TV programs, newspaper stories, stories from photographs. But this is too far into *my* story. Perhaps I should begin at the beginning.

In the Beginning . . .

Majella taught year 7 at my daughter's school in Australia, and she had asked me if I could do some storytelling with her class. I had done a lot of storytelling at schools, as well as teaching storytelling courses at my university. I knew that children of all ages enjoy listening to stories, but I wanted the children to be given the opportunity to start telling stories themselves. There was already so much listening by students to teachers in our schools that it seemed to me it was time for the teachers to start listening to their students! Storytelling provides the ideal context for genuine listening and talking exchanges.

So with these few goals in mind I embarked on the great voyage into the unknown. How would the children take to the idea of getting them to tell stories? What would I do if I were met with a cold resistance, or worse, indifference? Where would I begin?

I began with a story. I told "The Yellow Ribbon." It wasn't the story I had intended to tell, but when Majella introduced me to the class, I was met with faces full of uncertainty, suspicion, and indifference. I told the children that I would like to tell them a story, and immediately one boy threw down the challenge, "I hope it's a scary one." This signaled the others to join in a chorus of "Yeah, a really scary one." Some of the girls protested and said they liked funny stories better. So I decided that it had to be "The Yellow Ribbon," as it was both scary and funny.

At the end of the story I saw that the magic had worked. The children had dropped their defenses and talked animatedly about the story, how it made them feel, parts they enjoyed best, and so on. We were on our way. I told the class that for the next nine weeks I would be visiting their classroom every Friday and that we would be telling each other stories. This prompted all sorts of questions and comments: "What kinds of stories?" "Where do you get your stories from?" "It would be too hard." "Too embarrassing." "Other kids will laugh." "My voice is too soft." And so on. In fact, they reacted very much in the same way that my adult students do when I tell them that they are going to be storytellers. I reassured the children that they were already storytellers; every day they tell stories about things that have happened to them: they gossip, they relate last night's TV show, they tell jokes. All I was going to do was to show them some of the tricks of the professional storyteller's trade: ways of remembering stories they have read, how to adapt stories for oral retelling, ways of engaging with an audience, and how to find stories to tell.

Towards a Community of Storytellers

We started with personal stories. I had made my own personal storyboard, which consisted of a piece of paper divided into eight boxes. In each box I drew a picture of something that reminded me of a story from different stages of my life. I showed the class my storyboard and asked them to pick a picture. Then I proceeded to tell the story behind the picture. After each story, the talk followed in the form of questions, observations, hypotheses, extrapolations. Not a story told was left with a "so what" kind of response.

These stories about my life were not exciting tales of fighting lions in an African jungle or abseiling off Mount Everest; they were simple, everyday stories about growing up in Brisbane, Australia. They were familiar stories and each story sparked off something in each child's mind. For some, my story reminded them of a similar story that happened to themselves. For others, it was the sensation that the story gave them, and they spoke of how they would feel or react in a similar situation.

The children then produced their own storyboards and shared their stories of favorite birthday presents, of broken promises, of hidden fears, of joyous adventures, of family holidays, of unusual relatives, and so on.

When the children shared their stories, there were no uninterested listeners, no boring tellers, no embarrassment, no ridicule. We had revealed things about ourselves, and we were all getting to know each other better as people and not just as teachers and students.

After the personal-experience stories, we moved on to finding folktales to retell. Folktales are the ideal starting point for storytelling because they provide a fairly familiar structure, often incorporate repetition, are usually fairly short, and have a minimal number of characters. Majella and her class invaded both the school library and the local public libraries. Some children brought books from home libraries. The search for finding the right story began in earnest. An important spinoff from storytelling is that one needs to read a lot of books before one finds the story that one wants to tell. If we had mentioned this to several of the reluctant readers in the class, they may have balked at the idea, but by our not mentioning it they didn't realize that they had been hooked. All children, good readers and underconfident readers, read with an enthusiasm that Majella had not witnessed before. They could see that their reading had a purpose. Many skills such as skimming, locating, comparing, and evaluating were used instinctively by the children in their endeavors to locate the best version of a favorite folktale.

When the children had settled on their stories to retell, I showed them a number of strategies for helping them remember the events of the story and significant language. Trying to convince many of the children that storytelling is not reciting a story verbatim was difficult. Others, however, would quite readily dismiss the language of the written story and replace it with their own modern-day vernacular, which often did nothing for the integrity of the original tale.

Many children preferred to draw the key events of their stories on a storyboard or to map the sequence by using a story map. Some chose to list the sequence in short phrases, while others told a story on audiotape and played it over and over, making changes they felt were necessary. Once shown the different ways to learn a story, the children soon found the method that best suited their learning style.

Learning to tell a story takes time and requires plenty of opportunities to "talk out" the story. Keeping the story in one's head is only part of the process. Storytellers need to give voice to the words in their heads. They need to hear how the words sound, when to pause, which gestures to use, how to experiment with the voice to make some words soft, some loud, some slow, and some fast. We found that using peer tutors helped during this stage. In pairs, children would take turns in telling each other their stories and offering helpful suggestions for improving the presentation.

Sharing Our Stories

On Fridays when I was with the class, we worked on our formal storytelling presentations. We listened, offered advice, made changes, until we felt we had fairly polished oral retellings. The children decided to invite all the year 4 children to their classroom for a storytelling morning. Two storytellers were responsible for a group of five children and told the group their stories. This strategy helped to allay any fear or stage fright and gave confidence to the tellers and intimacy to the occasion. Then everyone enjoyed a special morning tea catered by the children in Majella's class.

On the other days of the week Majella and the children participated in a number of different storytelling situations of a more informal nature. Photographs were brought from home and their stories shared. A realia table of interesting items—an old rusty key, a tattered sun hat, a collection of shells and stones, an unusually shaped bottle, a baby's shoe—was used as a stimulus for telling stories.

Another Beginning

At the end of the ten weeks I asked the children what they thought of their storytelling experiences. All the children responded very favorably, and the overwhelming consensus was for more storytelling next term.

I went home after that last session with the words of Sean (twelve years) still ringing in my ears: "Storytelling is really good because when you're up there in the chair and telling to an audience it gives you confidence in yourself." If storytelling can give children confidence in themselves, then this in itself is high recommendation for its permeation throughout the curriculum.

But now I had next term to think about. What would I do? Where would we go from here? What if the children become bored with storytelling? Where would I begin?

I began with a story.

Acknowledgments

A fellow storyteller, Meg Philp-Paterson, gave me the idea for the personal storyboard, for which I am most grateful. To Robyn Clarke and Lyn Linning for their helpful suggestions.

4 Tell Me That One; Now Let's Tell It Together: Sharing Stories with Tim

Ann M. Trousdale

I was born into a family of storytellers, southern folk whose summer days drew to a close under the steady hum of a ceiling fan on the wide front porch, where we would sit as the grown-ups recounted for one another the day's events. In the way of born storytellers, they recast the day's happenings as stories, humorous or telling encounters with an array of fascinating if familiar small-town characters.

In the winter months, we would gather before the fireplace in my grandparents' bedroom, and after talk of the day, the stories would often turn to accounts of hunting trips, of memorable dogs or other colorful hunting companions.

"Uncle Bud, tell us again how Crookette got her name!" And the story of Crookette's broken tail would be followed by other reminiscences, often stories of our parents' or grandparents' childhood, tales familiarly comfortable enough to ease us into a sleepy sense of peace.

It was not surprising, then, that when I came to know young Tim and began to enjoy spending time with this three-year-old in the midst of weekend visits with his parents, I fell naturally into telling him stories about my own life events. It wasn't long before Tim was asking me to retell the stories which he had heard before: "Tell me the story about the time your kitten climbed the tree and wouldn't come down," or "Tell me about the time Christopher and David were visiting you and it froze and all your pipes broke and the electricity went out. Tell me that one."

Much of the information in this chapter was published in another form in *Language Arts* (1990), 67(2):164–173. The chapter also contains information not included in the *Language Arts* article.

My storytelling with Tim was different from my own childhood experiences with adults' storytelling; I was the only adult who was telling and Tim was the only child listening. He was the sole audience for these stories. But it wasn't long before he became more than audience. As Tim became increasingly familiar with the stories, he began to take over parts to tell himself. A pause in the tale of Susannah's tree-climbing escapade prompted Tim to supply, "Yeah, and then you got the ladder and climbed up it and called her and she still wouldn't come down."

As time went on, Tim began to take over other parts to tell. I was charmed by his desire to tell these stories with me; and sensing this I think, Tim began to take his turns with greater and greater confidence. Soon he began to elaborate on particular elements and to find ways to bring himself into the story itself as a participant, not just as a teller but as a participant in the action: "And then Tim the fireman came with his hook and ladder, climbed up, and got Susannah out of the tree." Tim the fireman also came along and repaired the damage to my electrical wires caused by the freeze, thus restoring heat and light to the house for Christopher, David, and me. Soon our storytelling was understood to be a cooperative venture, and the story lines became more and more unpredictable as Tim found ways to bring in surprising new twists.

I introduced Tim to the folktale "Jack and the Beanstalk," telling it to him rather than reading it. He listened enthralled as Jack's adventures unfolded. The story soon became his favorite, and on every visit he asked me to tell the story at least once. One morning as I was telling the story at the breakfast table and was about to describe how the beanstalk grew, Tim stood up in his chair and held his hand out close to the table top, then higher and higher, as the beanstalk grew and grew. Tim sat back down and listened until we reached the giant's first "Fe-fi-fo-fum, I smell the blood of an Englishman." Here Tim joined right in with me, and in Jack's next two encounters with the giant, I paused and Tim spoke the giant's lines alone. The story of "Jack and the Beanstalk" was never the same after that.

The next time I told the story, when I came to the place when Jack takes the cow to town to sell her but meets an old man on the road, I was surprised to hear from my little friend, "And that old man was *Tim*," who gave Jack the magic beans in exchange for the cow. Again Tim fell silent, and I continued the story. However, when Jack was about to climb up the beanstalk, suddenly his new friend Tim appeared and offered to go with him. I incorporated Tim into the story, and both of them went up the beanstalk and then to the giant's house. From that time on, Tim inserted himself into the story as a character and also took over segments to tell himself. He began to elaborate on incidents, introducing characters and elements from other stories familiar to him and solving problems in unique ways.

I had not realized that Tim was upset when Jack's mother punished him for selling the cow for a handful of beans rather than getting the money she had asked for. But very soon in his collaborating on the telling of the story, Tim had his character give Jack the magic beans *and* ten dollars for the cow. Thus when Jack got home, his mother was satisfied, Jack was not punished—and the adventure up the beanstalk was retained. Tim was always careful to include the money as part of the transaction after that.

Tim brought characters from other adventure stories to his tellings of "Jack and the Beanstalk." In one telling of the story, Superman appeared as the ultimate savior of Tim and Jack, killing the giant after they had escaped down the beanstalk for the last time. In the next telling, however, Tim became Superman himself, changing into his Superman suit behind a handy bush. (As an afterthought, he offered a Batman suit to Jack.) In this telling, Tim "zapped the giant with the magic zap from his fingers" and "zapped the beanstalk" at the end of the story as well. Superman and Batman became mainstays of the story.

Tim was moving with greater and greater ease from listener to participant in these tellings. Soon our storytelling took on the flavor of a dialogue. Our sessions became so interesting to me that I began to audiotape them. Following is a transcription of one of our later tellings of the story:

A: So he went over to that great big house and knocked on the door.

T: Boom!

A: Boom! Boom! In a minute the door opened, and this great big lady opened the door!

T: And she said, she looked around and she looked down there, and it was Tim and Jack.

A: She said, "Well, how're you doing?" She said, "I'll tell you one thing. You sure had better clear out of here, because if my husband sees two boys around his place, he'll eat you for supper."

T: And he said, "Oh, no, he won't, 'cause I gotta ask ya something. Is he afraid of Super Friends?"

A: "Super Friends?" she said. "I don't know if he's afraid of Super Friends, 'cause I don't think he ever heard of Super Friends."

T: "Well, they're some people that are super 'cause they save things."

A: "I see."

T: "And I brang the Superman, the Superman suit and the Batman suit for me and him."

A: "Oh, well, in that case, if you have a Superman suit and a Batman suit maybe you can come in, and I can give you a little bit of something to eat and you won't be afraid of the giant."

T: "Or maybe the giant will be afraid of *us*."

A: "That's right," she said.

T: "So maybe we could just hide somewhere and when we hear him—and when we hear some talkin' around here we'll come out. Maybe that's a good idea."

A later portion of the same transcription revealed to me to what an extent Tim was taking over major events to tell, elaborating on them or transforming them, while what I seemed to be doing was accepting his contributions, waiting until he had followed a train of thought as far as he could take it, and then returning to the basic story line.

A: So the giant lady persuaded him to sit down and have his supper. Which he did. Pretty soon . . .

T: They heard, "Snnnr! Snrr-brrr!" And then they sneaked out of the pie safe.

A: They sneaked out of the pie safe . . .

T: And he was counting his gold and he fell asleep and he wasn't counting his gold anymore. So Tim climbed up and got the gold.

A: And out of the house . . .

T: And, and Jack jumped on Superman's back and down Tim flew . . .

A: Until they got down to Jack's house.

T: And, and Tim gave Jack all the gold and mon—the gold was really more money.

A: Yes, it was.

T: And Tim flew off. And flew up to where the beanstalk was and got, and he just went like this with his big

> kryptonite beam and wham! threw the kryptonite beam on
> the giant's beanstalk and then it started to creak! Crrrr!
> And up there the giant was startin' to—uh! uh! Creak!
> Creak!

Tim's ending to this story has the giant come down the beanstalk,
find Jack's mother and eat her, then fall into the sea and get eaten by
a shark. Tim ended the story:

> T: So they put on their skeleton suits and they saw the giant
> on the bottom of the sea fighting with a great big shark.
> They went down to see, cut open the shark's belly, and
> there was the giant in the shark. And they cut open the
> *giant's* tummy and there was a woman.

I decided to introduce a new story to Tim, continuing to tape-
record our sessions. I adapted Richard Chase's retelling of the mountain
variant of "The Brave Little Tailor," a Jack Tale called "Jack and the
Varmints" (Chase 1943). My experience with "Jack and the Beanstalk"
had led me to expect that it would take several tellings before Tim
began to enter into the telling with me, but I was mistaken; once he
had a sense of the pattern of the story he jumped right in.

In the version I adapted from Chase's story, Jack swats seven
flies that land in his honey. He's proud of himself and makes himself
a belt that says, "Mighty Man Jack, Killed Seven at a Whack." The
king sees the belt, assumes Jack is very strong, and sets before him
three difficult deeds: ridding the mountains of a boar, a unicorn, and
a lion. With the help of good fortune, Jack is successful and is rewarded
by the king.

As I began telling the story, Tim commented on particular
elements, such as the likelihood that the flies and the honey would
get stuck to the flyswatter when Jack hit them with it, a problem that
had to be resolved before we went on.

Soon the wild boar came charging at Jack; Tim supplied loud
snorting noises. The pattern was repeated with the unicorn; Tim
whinnied and snorted. But during these first two episodes he was
essentially listening and participating in a minimal way. When we
came to the third task, however, Jack's confrontation with the lion,
Tim apparently felt comfortable enough with the story's pattern to
begin to offer contributions to the story line itself. Never having heard
the entire story, the events he related did not follow the traditional
plot, in which the lion trees Jack, Jack steps on a rotten branch and
falls on the lion's back, is afraid to get off the lion, and so rides the

raging lion into town where the lion is shot. Here is the version that unfolded between us:

> *A:* Jack sees a sycamore tree, skinnies up the sycamore tree real fast and there's that lion, comes to the bottom of the tree snarlin' and prowlin' around . . .
>
> *T:* I know what lions can do. You know what lions can do? They can go, they can go [makes scratching gestures].
>
> *A:* That's right. And that's exactly what he was doing to the bottom of that tree. Tryin' to scratch it down and gnaw it in two so the tree'd fall down and he could get Jack. Well, the lion pretty soon got tired. Fell down by the bottom of the tree, decided to take a little nap. Curled up at the bottom of the tree . . .
>
> *T:* Yeah, I bet he curled up like that [lies down in fetal position].
>
> *A:* He did. Curled up like that and fell asleep. Jack, he was lookin' down at that lion from the branch he was on, tryin to see . . .
>
> *T:* And I bet, I bet he found, he broke, um, a stick up on that sycamore tree and it was sharp and came down, down, um, the tree and keew! Put the sharp point of the stick in the lion.
>
> *A:* In the lion?
>
> *T:* Yeah.
>
> *A:* That would be a good thing to do all right, and then what would happen?
>
> *T:* He would be dead and he could take the other, um, um, end of the branch and pick it up and wheew! throw it into a real trap place.
>
> *A:* Right.
>
> *T:* So if he got the stick out and he was still alive he would be trapped.
>
> *A:* Yes.
>
> *T:* But he could scratch the door out.
>
> *A:* Yes. [pause] And then what would happen? Then what would Jack do next?
>
> *T:* I don't know.
>
> *A:* Well, Jack goes down the mountain . . . [picks up the story and continues, using Tim's additions]

Tim found his way into this episode through imitating the lion's gestures and movements, but his experience in shaping the stories we had told together apparently gave him the confidence to step right into this story, to begin shaping events himself, inventing problems and solving them, until he invented one he had no solution for. But that's all right; all storytellers run out of ideas sometimes.

This tradition of shared storytelling went on for about two years. When he was four, Tim began to initiate the same kind of interactive storytelling at bedtime, after his book had been read to him. He would typically ask his parents, or me if I was the one doing the reading, to "*tell* a story now." Once this pattern was established, he would often begin the new story himself. He would begin with a cast of characters, always including himself, place them in some kind of situation, introduce a conflict—and then, often, wait for the adult to further the plot. The direction of events was increasingly determined by Tim; the adult participation seemed to be invited more for the pleasure of the shared event than for a need to have solutions supplied. By the time he was five, Tim was successfully providing satisfactory conclusions to his stories.

At this time Tim was also exploring the written mode. One day when I arrived, his mother handed me a book Tim had written and illustrated for me. It was the story of David and Goliath. Despite his inability to spell the words he wanted to use (he was not at that time an inventive speller and asked his mother for the spellings), he had maintained the story line throughout the laborious process of writing it out. Included in Tim's story were the introduction of the characters, the conflict, and the resolution.

When Tim was six, I gave him an audiocasette recording of Richard Chase telling the Jack Tales. Occasionally he would ask to hear these stories at bedtime. One day, several months after I had given him the cassette, he asked his parents and me, "Would anybody like to hear a story?" He proceeded to tell, from beginning to end, the story "Jack and the Robbers," the mountain variant of "The Bremen Town Musicians." It is a highly complex and detailed story. Richard Chase's telling takes twenty-five minutes; Tim's took about fifteen, but he included every major element. Quite a storyteller, for a six-year-old.

I was impressed with how this kind of interactive storytelling had seemed to provide a bridge for Tim into an early ability to shape narrative independently. I had worked with Tim individually, but I wondered whether there were ways to translate interactive storytelling into the classroom, where one teacher was dealing with a number of children. I asked a first-grade teacher if I could come to her class to experiment with some ideas I had. Some of these ideas worked better than others, but all were successful on some level.

I worked with the whole class initially. I began with "The Little Red Hen," a story the children were familiar with in the basal-reader version. My version was more highly elaborated in both language and characterization than the version they knew, and so I told it to them once. Then I asked them to supply sound effects on a second telling and encouraged them to join in with me on the frequently repeated lines "Not I" and " 'Then I will,' said the little red hen." This they did with great delight.

Next I brought out stuffed animals: a dog, a cat, a mouse, and a hen. I asked for volunteers to "be" these characters, to say the characters' lines and to hold the animal whose part they were to take, while I was to "tell" or narrate the story. With a bit of initial prompting this went very well. Holding the stuffed animals seemed to give the children a sense of identity with the characters, as well as a sense of security in having something to hold onto.

Next I asked them to take turns telling the story. I brought out a Koosh ball that was to be passed from teller to teller, and a bell to signal when it was time to pass the ball to another child to continue the story. I began the story, then rang the bell and passed the Koosh ball to one child. That child continued the story and, when I rang the bell, passed it to another child. The rule was that it had to be passed to someone who had not had a turn before.

I noticed that the Koosh ball was passed several times to a little Chinese girl, who would take it, then immediately pass it along to someone else. But several children, after taking their turn, passed it back to her. Finally, at the very end, she kept the ball when it was passed to her and brought the story to its conclusion, very charmingly. Her teacher told me later that that was the child's first oral participation in a class activity. Such is the power of shared storytelling.

I have also divided classes into small groups for more independent storytelling after telling the story in the large group. In small groups children can work with the stuffed animals, with a Koosh ball or a beanbag, or with masks of story characters, involving more children in the telling of the story. The children's personal involvement in the stories and their enjoyment of the tellings is obvious.

My experience with Tim and with using this kind of interactive storytelling in elementary classrooms has convinced me of several things. First, that through inviting children into the process of telling stories—retelling familiar stories or creating new ones—we foster their confidence in themselves as storytellers and thus give them confidence in their emergent narrative abilities in significant ways. Second, such invitations to explore narrative, to elaborate, to invent, to take risks with new episodes are invitations to enter the story-making world itself. When children develop an understanding of what a story is from the inside out, by creating or helping to create the story world themselves, the process becomes not remote, but immediate, their own. Such storytelling provides children with the kind of authority that comes with personal knowledge, and the kind of self-confidence that is gained through repeated experiences of success.

5 The Journey of One Young Storyteller

Marni Schwartz

2/23 Dear L.L.

My story is dum!!! I'm not a good write at all. I don't spend a lot of
on writing because I don't write good. I don't want to say it aloud.
It sounds dull. I don't have an more to write.

This is the first entry in Sally's storytelling learning log (L.L.). A day or
two earlier, storyteller Jeannine Laverty had told my sixth-grade
students a Cheyenne tale which included many unexplained or
magical elements, one being an immortal double-toothed bull. Afterward,
Laverty directed us in the creating of original tales to explain how one of
those elements came to be. I decided on the use of the learning log, hoping
it would help the children prepare their tales for telling and give me some
insights into their learnings about this art of storytelling.

Sally had already shown me again and again how little confidence
she had in herself as a language learner. Each time she faced a new task
she reminded me, "I've never been good in English." Though her middle
school class contained a heterogeneous mix of sixth graders, she had had
enough experience in ability groups to believe school success belonged to
others, not to her. The log now offered a chance to voice her anger and fear
of inadequacy on paper.

How We Used the Learning Log

My introduction of the log went something like this: Our logs are a
place we can write about successes or difficulties we meet creating a
new tale from Jeannine's. Then as we continue the unit and look for
our own stories in books or on tapes, we can write about the ups and
downs of that. We might describe how we rehearse, for there are
many ways to practice a story. We might write about how some stories
are alike or how versions of stories differ from each other. The log
will be a place to figure out storytelling or "talk" about what we have
figured out about it.

Each student wrote or at least outlined an original tale suggested by Laverty's telling. I had done storytelling units before but had not asked students to create tales. Laverty took us through activities such as silent visualizing of or fantasizing about our stories. We listed the key events and characters and drew maps of the landmarks in our stories, using arrows for movement and symbols or letters for characters. Everyone added small but clear sensory details to make the scenes or characters more visible to listeners. We played with voice inflections to create mood, added bits of conversation to establish a sense of the characters, and incorporated gestures to suggest the size of an object or person or the direction or speed of movement. You might say we drafted and revised both the stories and our tellings as we worked through these activities. I encouraged students simply to "keep writing" in the log about what was happening.

Later in the unit, students chose a story for telling from some written or recorded source. We signed out folktale books from our middle school library, borrowed picture books from the public library, and dug our own favorite collections from childhood days out of boxes in attics or retrieved them from the primary classrooms of parents who were teachers. My goals were to have students both read folk literature and tell a tale before an audience.

A Few Log Entries

Sally's second entry just a day later shows, though she's still scared, she wants to be a part of what this unit promises. Some students had rehearsed "drafts" of their original tellings before the class.

> 2/24 Dear L.L.
>
> I wish I could write storys like Brian, Joey, Diane, etc. I'm not going to say it aloud.

Other student entries show some of the variety of responses. One of the things I had asked them to consider was how they went about preparing their tellings. They were free to write throughout the period as students tried stories aloud. Ben, who in the fall told me, "I stink at writing" (mostly, I discovered, because his handwriting was nearly illegible), articulated several discoveries in his log after observing that first day's rehearsals:

> I ask how to "beef up" the beginning were tooth [the double-toothed bull] was born. The map and motions helped. Overall

I think it was easy. Tonite I will practice telling it to my parents.
It seams that a lot are short.

More and more I'm finding copy-cat storys.

I now realize that using facial expressions and voice is the best
way to tell a story.

Telling in tandem is neat how you can swich dialoge and have
quick action tellings.

I could change the dialect in any story.

Christine, on the other hand, had perfect penmanship and read
between thirty and fifty books each marking period. She seemed to
enjoy writing but read her piece aloud to the class only when required:

The way I prepared for my story was just to read it (aloud in
my head.) My story reminds me of something that I've either
read or seen before, but I can't really place it. I'm not very
happy with it it's just, well dumb! I don't mind reading for a
few friends but other people make me nervous, but I guess if
they don't like it that's their problem. None of the other stories
were that good except the teacher's.

The best exercise Jeannine gave me was writing my story in
short steps. Then I saw my basic story.

Brian, in contrast to Christine, loved performing of any kind.
He volunteered for any dramatic activity, and his unsolicited performances, both in and out of the classroom, always gained both his
peers' and teachers' attention. Laverty sensed this and included him
in the first day's public rehearsals. These are his first entries:

I got the idea by just wondering how it would work. I decided
to make it so I could have fun telling it.

When that lady came and made me go up thier I was in the
process of eliminating parts. When I was up there I wanted to
sit down but when I started to tell my story it pulled me to
keep on going.

When the next story telling assignment comes I hope it's more
exciting.

My question was why did I like the others better than mine.

I enjoyed doing this project because it helped to develop my
creativity.

Those student reactions show how even at the unit's beginning
the young storytellers consciously stepped into the processes of trying

on a tale and working with it both as a public performance for classmates and teacher and as a learning experience for themselves.

Surrounding Students with Story

When it came time for students to choose a tale, we spent several class periods reading and searching for powerful tales. Some students reached for old favorites, while others seemed amazed at the wealth of tales they never knew existed. The picture books brought from basements and attics added a musty smell to the room, as well as childish giggles and various forms of "Oh, remember this?" We hunted up audio- and videotapes from the growing supply in local bookstores and libraries. And I told a variety of my favorite fables, poems, and family stories. I wanted children to see the possibilities in storytelling material and styles.

Some students, drawn to a complicated written tale, struggled to become confident with the twists and turns of their stories. Others found very short written versions which would need some "meat on their bones" to become lively tellings. Some students abandoned a tale quickly; others stayed with a story until near deadline before jumping ship. We discovered that the lessons learned in shaping one telling transferred to the next. Everyone was "ready" once the first round of tellings began.

More Than One Kind of Discovery

Throughout the unit, I insisted that students read widely. I required everyone to keep a list of various sources, a brief summary of each story read, and some personal response in a back section of the log. This backfired. Students who indeed read widely—Christine, for instance—considered this busywork. It cut down on their reading and it reduced, I sensed too late, the comments they made in the process section of the log. Few students noticed motifs such as the youngest lucky-in-the-end brother or magic pots. Only one or two wrote about how animal stories are "really people stories if you read them with that in mind." The entries in the logs seemed to be written with the childlike joy of discovery. The summaries and personal responses were written in the flat tone common to book reports.

This record keeping backfired in other ways. Students who were lingering with certain tales or already working on the telling which they knew was ahead simply copied names of stories they knew but hadn't read just to meet my "read widely" expectation. Sally, who had unearthed her old Br'er Rabbit picture-book collection, after stumbling across one "Brother Rabbit" story in a picture book I had treasured as a child, hid her book daily, hoping I wouldn't notice she wasn't reading from any other texts. She dutifully listed every single tale and wrote responses such as: "I love Uncle Remus's stories." "It is Great!" "I like how Brer Rabbit is so smart." "I think Brer Rabbit is a little mean." "Thank God Brer Rabbit was their."

While I wanted to help all my students see the vast amount of folk literature and the number of children's books now available to them, I don't want a reading requirement to get in the way of what aspects of storytelling they will naturally pursue. I also discovered that the tellings themselves were the best advertisements for the treasures of folk literature there for the taking.

The Power of Stepping inside the Story

3/2 Dear L.L.

I changed my story alot. It's about how they [the Cheyenne brothers] got their names. I think I want to tell it alot. I didn't rehers a lot but I think it's good. I told it to my mom and dad they helped me get the names.

I like how she says it so slow.

I think the end of my story was funny. I think I said it O.K. But I don't use hand movements as much.

I like how Keven changed his vosie [voice]. What was it supposed to mean?

I feel better about my story now.

Those are Sally's entries on the day she told her original tale. She wrote them in one paragraph, but I separated them to show the attention she gave both her own tale and the tales of others who shared their stories that day.

After the original tellings, we set a few days aside for reading and searching, but that had been going on even as students were preparing their original stories. Sally's entries continue to show her growth:

3/10 Dear L.L.

I'm reading a folktale I love to read.

One day we devoted the forty-minute class to an exercise in which we divided the fable "The Boy Who Cried Wolf" into key events. Then we separated those events into the story's beginning, middle, and end. In groups of threes chosen randomly out of a hat, the children told the story. All the groups had a limited time to prepare simultaneously. Then each group had just a moment's conference time between tellings to make changes, smooth transitions, or simply coach each other toward a confident, if not very polished, telling. Sally got to tell the story's end when her group took its turn. Her excitement may be responsible for her forgetting to address L.L.:

> 3/14 We are having a lot of fun. I was scared to go up there but it was fun. It was scary up there I was really nerves. I didn't really know what to say for the moral.

All year Sally had been more comfortable with structured, well-defined assignments than with open-ended ones. She struggled to find writing topics even at this point in the year. I sensed that no one had ever or often asked her to generate ideas or tasks out of what she liked to do. The storytelling task was fairly well defined, but it allowed her to go to a familiar and therefore safe place for material:

> 3/19 Dear L.L.
>
> I like the story I'm going to tell. It's hard but I am going to tri. I like the story alot thats why I am so persistins. I think the list helped me a little I didn't really use it. I have to read the story over and over. Until I get the hang of it. I'm a little scared but I just have to get it. I love Uncle Remus storys they are my favorite.

I did not "catch" the next entry until after Sally had told her story:

> 3/23 Dear L.L.
>
> This is the last practising day. I changed my story last night. I changed it with my tutor and I changed because my first story was to long and comblicaded. My story I am doing now is shorter and not as hard.

March 23 turned out not to be the last practicing day for a number of reasons, much to Sally's and others' relief:

> 3/25 Dear L.L.
>
> I hate to practice in fornt of people because I'am neves. But I did practice a lot.

Once student telling began, we listened to all twenty-eight for several days. Between stories I took a picture of each teller in one dramatic pose from the story. Sally finally got her moment in the sun. No one wanted to be the first teller of the day, so I resorted to bribing: extra credit to go first:

> 3/30 Dear L.L.
>
> I can't belev that I did my story first. But it was extra credit. I was real nerve I could have died. But I did it.

> Dear Sally,
>
> Yes you did! What parts were *you* proudest of? "Those apples up there was REALLY GREEN and they weren't ready to fall!" That line really stood out for me. Your accent gave a wonderfully funny flavor to the tale. GLAD you had fun with this telling. Everyone enjoyed it. I could tell, could you? I'm really proud of your work, Sally. I'll always picture you when I think of Brer Rabbit from now on.
>
> MS

I had written little questions of encouragement in Sally's log before, but my note the day after her telling reflects her teacher's pride the way Sally's entry reflects hers.

My anecdotal records on Sally's progress show that she closed out sixth grade on this same high. She volunteered to tell two more stories from the collection (including the one she had prepared but abandoned), and she volunteered for a teamwide assembly of some of the most successful tellings—before an audience of more than one hundred middle schoolers and several teachers. Later in the spring during a poetry unit, Sally memorized a number of poems for performance, composed several poems about sports she likes, and on a self-evaluation of the unit wrote, "I know I can write a good poem if I try."

Through storytelling, she had come a long way from "My story is dum!!!"

6 Tap Your Storytelling Roots!

Joe Yukish

I donned my story shirt with the baggy sleeves, put on my flat top hat, and prepared to tell my story to my faculty colleagues gathered at the annual Christmas party. I was filled with insecurity. Tell a story to my colleagues? Would they care for a story? How could I deliver a story that would hold *their* interest? I'd been a fool to say I would do this. As I'd done so many times in the past, I allowed my fear of the situation to overshadow the strength I could draw from my past, from my storytelling roots.

For many years, I had been unaware of how much the rich background gleaned from growing up in a second-generation Slovak-Croatian family contributed to my ability to engage in storying with groups of any age or occupation. I had "forgotten" my early years in Appalachia as a coal miner's son, when my family had little money for recreation other than enjoying people and visiting each other. I had also "forgotten" that these visits provided interaction with real people, the slices of life from which stories are made.

My family was made up of a storying group of individuals that Brown (1991) describes as folks who took more joy in spending time visiting with others than people did in other parts of the country where lives were sped up. While visiting each other, they allowed room for verbal relaxation and an appreciation for the narrative art. Indeed, my people were a "storying lot" who showered every family member with tales, tales, and more tales.

Early in my teacher education training, my failure to appreciate the value of my roots may have resulted from that cocky elitism that often initially overshadows the thinking of the first in a family to pursue an advanced education. When I entered college, I was entering a level of education higher than that achieved by anyone else from either my mother's or father's families. My mother finished sixth grade before leaving to work for people in New York City as a maid. Most of her salary was sent back to her parents. My father interrupted two separate attempts at completing eighth grade so he could return to work in the coal mines earning money to help his family. The havoc of the Depression and the cost of feeding and clothing their children took precedence over my grandparents' desire for any of their children to earn an education.

My parents' lack of education, or the "provide for physical needs first" priorities that had been communicated to them by their parents, may have influenced the home environment they created for my sister and me. Books were not part of my childhood possessions, and we never used the library that was located in the town more than fifteen miles away. When I studied reading instruction in my teacher education courses, I silently apologized for my parents, feeling the guilt they did not know because they had never read a story to their children during our youth.

The same insecurities had haunted me in my earliest attempts at storytelling, just as they were to do years later at the faculty Christmas party. My first encounter with "formal" storytelling came during my undergraduate children's literature course, when Professor Marian Weaver required us to tell a story—without a book!—from memory!—to receive a grade in her course. I chose Robert Lawson's *Robbut: A Tale of Tails* (1989).

The night before I was to tell the story, overexposure to some unseasonably cold fall weather caused a ticklish feeling in my throat, while my self-doubt about being able to tell the story caused a whole swarm of butterflies in my stomach. Tell a story for Professor Weaver?—I can't do it. I don't know anything about telling stories. I just found this book about this rabbit a few weeks ago.

I tried a trip to Josephine's, but courage didn't come from socializing at the local pub. Trying to talk over the loud music to complain about my "tellin' task" on the next day only made my throat hurt more and my voice more raspy. On the way back to the dorm, much too early in the morning, I found a temporary solution to my dilemma. I screamed and yelled with my loudest voice in the crisp October air. By the time I returned to Johnson Hall, I could hardly talk. The morning brought a full-blown case of laryngitis, and a respite from telling the story.

Strained vocal cords do heal, however, and a week later I stood in front of Professor Weaver and the participants in my language arts course to tell Lawson's story. After I got the story started, I found that I took joy in the opportunity to tell about Robbut's discovery that his own tail was the best after all. Much to my surprise, it was easy for me to tell the story! I found I *could* "story"!

But if my youth was so deprived of literature, of reading stories, how could telling them come so easily to me? Recently, I've realized that one answer to this question comes from those hours I spent enjoying the verbal relaxation and narrative art, as Brown (1991) expresses it, during family visits. Mikkelsen (1990) describes the talk and stories that occur during such visits as "talk-story." She recommends that we transform our attitudes about these stories to see them as a source of literacy. Mikkelsen describes "talk-story" as "another literacy, a third literacy (the first literacy?). This literacy would be no less important than reading and writing, but instead a fundamental means for shaping and learning—not merely enriching, but vital for all" (565).

Visits with my family during these years occurred in the same settings as those so beautifully described by Cynthia Rylant in *The Relatives Came* (1985). Stories filled those moments, which became hours and even days without a book in sight. Tales from all my aunts as well as my momma about what it was like to raise a child alone while their husbands were overseas in World War II. Dialogues between sisters that explained why Mom chased Uncle J.Z. with a clothesline prop from Uncle John's wedding reception at Grandpap's house. (Uncle J.Z. had had too much to drink again!) Haunting tales about how the family members in Old Country (Czechoslovakia) felt a visit from the spirit of Grandma (my mother's mother) in their house on the very night of the day she died, before my aunts and uncles had been able to contact them to let them know that Grandma had passed away. All sorts of stories and tales that ranged from what it would be like if Uncle Youngstown would win big at Bingo, to why the blackberries used to make the pies we all loved were bigger and better when the people telling about the berries were children like us.

My roots in storytelling grew from hearing these tales and from the opportunities my cousins and I had to tell a few tales of our own. These relatives would listen to the stories of the children, and they even seemed to take joy in hearing from us. The story about Cousin Joey's and my attempts to snorkel the bottom of a deep, deep cove in Deep Creek Lake to recover the pole that was yanked from the boat by a "big'un" brought belly laughs from Uncle Jim. He knew the cove was so deep one would have trouble getting to the bottom of it with scuba gear. As he chuckled, he thought of another story about something just as silly, and then shared it. Weren't these experiences as valuable as being immersed in books? Maybe I can "story" because I grew up surrounded by storying people.

Earlier in the beginnings of my teaching career, when I was an elementary teacher, I really didn't value the importance of children's literature and making time for stories in the elementary curriculum. I was a "bound in the basal" reading teacher and did little to extend beyond the literature provided within the covers of those books. I would tell the Robert Lawson story I prepared for Professor Weaver once a year as a special treat. When I told this story, however, I didn't realize the joy that the children took in it or my joy in telling it. I read aloud to my students periodically.

But for me, literature was a frill that the children could choose to engage in outside the time I spent with them in math, workbooks, the spelling program, handwriting practice for the Peterson writing specimens that were due each month, and textbook studies.

The children's literature courses I took in graduate school opened a new world of teaching possibilities. I discovered the importance of sharing children's books and extending the classroom curriculum through children's literature. Yet even with the shifts taking place in my thinking, I still did not engage in storytelling, nor did I include it in the undergraduate special education and reading courses I was teaching. As Huck, Helper, and Hickman (1987) suggest, I probably neglected emphasizing storytelling in my teacher education courses because I felt there were too many beautiful books to share and because I sympathized with the teachers' harried lifestyle that allowed little time for "learning" stories to tell.

Besides, I asked myself, "How can I teach something I have never really done? Telling Robbut once a year does not a storyteller make!" Then I discovered that Karen Varaunch, an ex-theater major who worked in the college admissions office, took an interest in storytelling and was currently involved in developing the art. Without much coercion, Karen agreed to spend three, one-hour sessions in my undergraduate children's literature course and one, three-hour evening session in my graduate course.

Karen was wonderful! She told stories that my students could learn and try telling immediately, such as the "Tailor's Magic Cloth" (Shimmel 1982). She told more complex literary tales that would enthrall and amaze us. She shared storytelling tips and techniques and told us about how she expanded her knowledge of the art of storytelling through the National Association for the Perpetuation and Preservation of Storytelling (NAPPS) in Jonesborough, Tennessee.

Karen taught my college students so well that I, like Professor Weaver, could require them to tell a story. But I tried to make the experience more practical: I required them to tell their stories to a group of children at the elementary school across the street.

I had fulfilled the need for storytelling in my course! Karen visited my courses for several semesters. I was doing my job, providing a complete course in children's literature with storytelling included. Until—Karen Varaunch moved to the southern part of West Virginia.

Remaining true to my conviction of never trying to teach anything I have never done myself, I realized I could not take Karen's place in the storytelling module of the course until I made a serious attempt at trying my hand at storytelling. One fall afternoon, I talked to Steve Willikie, the principal of the school I used for the storytelling field experiences. "Steve, I need to tell some stories so I can teach my children's literature course. Karen left the college last summer." Steve agreed to give me a gig.

I chose to tell some stories taught by Karen, an Alvin Schwartz scary story called the "Viper" (1981), and "Budulinek," a Czechoslovakian-Polish story from my Eastern European ancestry, found in Arbuthnot's text *Children and Books* (1957, 351–353). I used a story apron, made by a friend, with pockets to hold pictures of Budulinek and other characters from his story. Velcro dots on the chest part of the apron enabled me to become a walking flannel board with Grandmother's succulent lunches, Budulinek, Lishka the fox, and the organ grinder.

I shook a bit at first, but discovered that I could "story" with these children and achieve a level of intimacy and interaction beyond that of reading books aloud. The group joined in telling certain parts of the story, just as Karen said they would. They repeated the colors of the Tailor's Magic Cloth in unison, with enthusiasm, and recited the "years, and years, and years" refrain with me, then stopped to hear the next part of the story, waiting for their next cue. The Budulinek story caused the children to shudder with fear when Lishka the fox entered the house. They were convinced that Viper was a vile, mean creature, and chuckled along with the teachers when they discovered that this viper wanted to do nothing more than "Vash and Vipe the Vindows." In those forty-five minutes, I went beyond developing the experience necessary to teach my course. I was smitten with a new desire—the desire to become a storyteller.

Steve called the next day to tell me I had "rave reviews." He invited me to visit again. Other principals took advantage of my quest, asking me to tell stories to their students. Wanting to enhance my skills, I read. Every book in the local library that dealt with storytelling had my signature on the library card that year. No courses dealing with storytelling were offered by the local universities, but I remembered Karen's discussions about NAPPS. I'd go there! I attended the NAPPS Annual Storytelling Festival in Jonesborough, Tennessee, that year and heard such master storytellers as The Folktellers, Jackie Torrence, Ed Stivender, Jay O'Callahan, Elizabeth Ellis, Doc McConnell, Mary Carter Smith, Kathryn Windham, Heather Forest, Laura Simms, and the legendary Ray Hicks. I now had a frame, a template through which to view what storying is all about. In the process, my desire to become a storyteller was changing to an obsession.

Over the next few years, I pursued my goal. I studied more; I practiced; I told stories to hundreds and then thousands of schoolchildren. I visited Jonesborough each summer for workshops, participating in seminars and workshops led by Jay O'Callahan, Barbara Freeman, Gioia Timpanelli, Diane Wolkstein, Carol Birch, Michael Parent, Doug Lippman,

Rafe Martin, and Augusta Baker. At the advice of my storying mentors, I told more stories to schoolchildren, to groups in public libraries, and to groups of adults in churches and civic groups. I conducted workshops on storytelling at young authors' conferences, trying to convince these budding authors that they too were storytellers. I provided inservice sessions for teachers on the art of storytelling and using storytelling as a springboard to writing. I presented storytelling sessions at regional conferences of the International Reading Association and NAPPS.

Storytelling became my avocation, while I maintained my vocation as a professor of reading instruction. Even though the demands of my professional vocation provided barriers to my devoting more time and energy to storytelling, my teaching career assisted me in finding the true value of stories. Training in the Reading Recovery Program at Ohio State University enabled me to study with Charlotte Huck, Gay Su Pinnell, Diane DeFord, and Carol Lyons, who led me to a greater appreciation of the role of literature and stories in the development of literacy. It was during this time that I finally began to appreciate my storytelling roots, to realize that my family and their tales upon tales had given us all experience with language through story, a form of communication that could cause wonder and happiness. I realized that, as Barton and Booth (1990) suggest, we are members of story tribes, a "part of the story tapestries of our tribes, our threads woven into yours, each tale embroidered with the strands of others, for all time" (174).

What effect did my storytelling have on the schoolchildren I told stories to? One incident stands out in my mind as an example of the infectious nature of storying with children. I was working at some landscaping in the back yard when Nick, my youngest son, brought his new friend Dan to meet me.

"I know you," Dan proclaimed, "You're that guy who said you had peanut butter in your mouth." Then, turning to Nick, he said, "Your dad tells good stories."

"What did he tell you besides the peanut butter one?" Nick asked.

"He told us this one about . . ."

Dan launched into telling the story to Nick, verbatim! Nick returned by telling his version of "Mary Culhane," a story he had heard me tell many times.

I continued to spade the flower bed thinking, "You're making storying happen, Yukish! You're making it happen!"

But storying isn't just for children. Older "kids," even sophisticated college faculty members, are subject to the spell of a good story. Five years later, in a new home in a new part of the country, I tested my storytelling wings at the faculty Christmas party. I was going to tell Rebecca Caudill's *A Certain Small Shepherd* (1965). Overcoming those familiar anxieties, I stepped onstage and began to tell the bittersweet tale. Again, the power of the story itself took over, and as I finished, a hush filled the room. Then the applause.

That I had brought that roomful of university faculty members into the world of the story was testified to by a note of appreciation from an esteemed colleague who had had his writing nominated for a Pulitzer Prize that year. He wrote,

> I was seated at the back table during both stories, and I absolutely marvelled at how you held that roomful of boisterous, party-minded adults in spellbound silence. And it just seemed to come so natural to you, effortless, with a graceful ease. Several times I noted couples looking at each other with that child-like kind of anticipation at certain points in the story—as only children can do.
>
> Somebody at our table noted that you got the longest applause of the evening and with good reason; you had worked a kind of magic that so many of us hadn't experienced in years, and it was wonderful. (Parks 1990)

II Making Connections: Discovering the Power of Storytelling in the Classroom

"The teachers I remember most are the ones who told us stories," a university student commented. "I still remember the stories they told."

"Yes," agreed a classmate, "and the only history that seems to have stuck with me was when stories made it come alive."

"But were you ever lucky enough to have teachers who let *you* tell stories?" asked a third. "That's when I really put things together!"

Since the beginning of time, stories have been used to make sense of experience, to inform others, to pass along information and values. In this section, you will encounter stories of storytelling from a wide range of classrooms, from elementary school to freshman year in college, from ESL classrooms to youth correctional facilities. The stories in this section also tell how storytelling can serve to develop self-awareness and self-confidence, to open windows of imagination into the past that illuminate the present, and to help us understand our present world and the people who inhabit it.

"May I tell you my story?" a young Russian immigrant asks. In Ruth Merrill's account, it is storytelling that breaks barriers of fear and alienation in an ESL classroom, as a folklore teacher encourages the students to bring their own family stories to school.

Sharon Kane's story is also told from a student's perspective. Her journal from a freshman composition class gives a humorous view of an unforgettable storyteller of a teacher, a teacher who is more canny about the power of storytelling than her students suspect. If you've never had a teacher who lured you into unexpected learning through telling stories, you'll encounter one here!

Both Barbara Connelly and Mary Murphy find that storytelling is able to reach students whom they could not otherwise entice into participation in class.

He "found somewhere to hang his hat," Barbara Connelly notes, as Andrew, a shy "invisible" child, finds success and even a touch of fame through a middle school storytelling club. What stands behind Andrew's emergence as a mesmerizing storyteller is a teacher who is sensitive enough to offer, to present the possibilities, and then to stand back and let storytelling do its work.

"Word up, Man," Edmund's peers exclaim as the fourteen-year-old boy finishes telling his story. Through Edmund, Mary Murphy discovers that storytelling in a youth correctional facility offers troubled students a chance to hear each other and be heard, to experience success in school, and an opportunity to face the stories they've lived.

It's no surprise that noted storyteller Syd Lieberman uses storytelling in his high school English classes. Here he recounts how storytelling helped one high school writer discover the heart of her piece. Syd has found that, for students whose compositions appear flat in early draft form, storytelling can add the needed dimensions of sight, sound, and emotion.

From a parent's perspective, Tom Romano tells how the seeds of his father's immigration tales grew into a powerful fictional story told by his daughter, Mariana, for her high school English research project. Through Mariana's story, set in 1914, we see how we can come to know the past through story and how that knowledge can form the material for written narratives as well.

Finally, Barbara Lipke gives us highlights of almost twenty years of using storytelling in education—storytelling on trains in China, in bilingual and special education classes, from prekindergarten through sixth-grade levels. Through Kathy, Irit, and others we see how storytelling transformed Barbara's teaching and brought learning to life for her students.

Tune in to the tellers, the tales, and the listeners. Whether or not the learning environment is defined by the four walls of a schoolroom, you will hear how teachers and students, both tellers and listeners, make discoveries that give them a deeper understanding and acceptance of themselves and each other.

7 May I Tell You My Story?

Ruth Merrill

Have you time, may I tell you my story? I am a student from Russia and my family immigrated to the United States. In my country, there were many nights around the kitchen table that I heard the grown-ups, my parents, all the family, and neighbors discussing going to America. It was many imaginations and many talks. I had an aunt, and her family was ready to go too. She was old, short, and funny. She thought that in America you do not have to work, just push the button and all is going to be in your house. We just laughed at her. We thought America is big, people are walking around in brilliant clothes, and the food is delicious. I always wanted to go and eat fruits, like oranges, pineapples, all kinds of fruits. We thought that American people are very smart and they have all kinds of things, like cars, instruments for music, and toys. So we thought America is like a different land. We really did not know anything about this land.

I understand the talk of leaving was something very dangerous to discuss. For many years, our family had been applying for visas. For many years we had been turned down. We saved every ruble, we did without. More and more we thought we were watched. Our mail opened and resealed, the trash was studied, fear was our constant companion. It seemed like forever, because it was so frightening.

Suddenly, the money my father made was, for no reason, cut. The family thought the only way to leave was to abandon the endless government channels—to escape. It was like the wind that finally bent the willow. The talk lasted longer into the night. Then, we could not believe it, our visas were approved. The plans were made, we would go to America.

But then there were months in the relocation camp. Other people at the camp had letters from relatives in America. The writing was almost gone from the many times the letters were opened, read, cried

---

This is a story that teacher Ruth Merrill has written in one voice, drawing together the stories of five ESL students—Adriana, Sone, Galina, Mikela, and Bountom—whom she taught during her master's program.

over, folded carefully, and put away. There were people from many countries, many with stories too sad to tell. Finally, word came we were to leave.

When we came to America, a kind woman who spoke our language was waiting for us at the airport. Everyone squeezed into the car. We were on our way to a new home. I remember the woman was trying to explain about the seat belts when there was a terrifying alarm sound. My father began to pray. We all knew we were caught. We sat there in the car with our hands up waiting for the police. The woman was confused, but then the seat belt alarm stopped. She apologized. We wondered how we would get along in this strange, noisy place without her. We were tired but we were home.

The next day the interpreter came to our house to take us to shop at a market. It was beautiful. There were mountains of oranges. "Revolution" was an English word my father learned. "Revolution" is all he could say to show his feelings. In our country, we had oranges only if our mother stood in line once for one orange, again for the second, then on to the next line for bread. The sights, sounds, and people made us weary and we were happy to go back to our little house. Saravana, our interpreter, said next week I would begin school. I thought about all my dreams and wondered what it would be like.

On my first day of school, a counselor took me to what they called a homeroom. I was so scared I cried. I could not look up from my desk. The teacher was speaking, but I could not understand him. I heard him say my name but he did not pronounce it correctly. Suddenly, a bell sounded. Everyone started leaving. What did it mean? Where were they going? I just stayed in my chair because in Russia we do not change classes. I saw the counselor in the hall, pointing at me, waving at me. I was afraid I would cry again. I did not understand why he wanted me to move because I thought my teachers would come to me. I wanted someone to tell me what to do. But no one spoke my language. I thought I could never learn English.

Now I have been at school for a year. My teacher says I am very good at English, but there is still so much to learn. I am in six classes and I have a special English teacher. There are five other refugee students from Laos, Vietnam, and Romania. We meet for lunch together. I am meeting some other people, but it is slow and lonely at times. The students are cold. Sometimes, I even wish for my old home. Papa will not hear of such talk. At his work they tell him he must improve his English or maybe lose his job. Mama does not speak

English, so I shop, make the phone calls, and sometimes I want just to be a kid. But I am glad to help my family.

A few weeks ago there was another teacher. She was happy, warm, with a smile even in her eyes. She said she was excited and privileged to work with us. She wanted us to know about folklore. She had a box of library books. They were stories from all of our countries. There were stories I knew as a child. They were in English, but I could show them to my friends, our dress and customs, and my favorite story when I was little. We could even take them home. I took two home to read with my little brother to help him with his English.

The teacher said she would be back. When she returned she talked with us about making our own stories, our own folklore. We complained we had no stories to tell. She laughed and told us a story about herself. She called it a rough draft and showed us how she was editing it. We even helped her. She called it cooperative learning. We could interview our parents for stories too. I told her my father had many, many stories but he does not have enough words to tell them. The teacher just asked us to try. We did not have to worry about spelling or grammar, it was for us, for our children.

One of the students from Laos, Sone, did not yet speak English, so the teacher sat with her, drawing pictures, interviewing her about her family, favorite foods, herself. It was Sone's first writing in English. Bountom, another student from Laos, told her that when she had been here longer, it would not be so hard or scary.

Then Bountom told her story of flight from Laos to Thailand. It was difficult for her to put into words, that night of escape. We all helped her to write the story. Bountom told how they took only the clothes they had on. None of the kids knew where they were going. She told us of squatting, cramped inside the basket, sweating and numb yet frigid with fear. Her baby sister hushed, would they make it? No one uttering what might happen to them if they were caught. Finally, the sound of the truck stopping at the border checkpoint, they were all holding their breath. But the truck lurched and the night was pierced by the baby's startled cry. The shouts of the guard, the lid snatched off the basket, the lights blinding. She told how her father was calm, he said they were going to visit their family. Her father gave the guards all their money that was hid in their clothes. It was their only money, their savings. A miracle, the guard closed the lids, pushed the baskets close together, and they went into Thailand, into the city.

The teacher cried, just a little, and hugged us. She told us that a teacher is very fortunate because of all she gets to learn. I decided to write the other stories. The stories help me see how far I have come and someday they might help someone else. I have lots of other writing to do in school. There is the paper about *Moby Dick* and next week I am to do an oral report on antiaircraft missiles. I have to stand in front of the class and read it. I may not come to school that day.

The teacher who worked with the stories is gone. She writes to us; she is studying to be a teacher of English for refugees. Our little group is very close, I think because we shared our stories. We are all keeping journals and writing, working on some of our stories. Next year we will go to different high schools, but we promise to keep in touch. Someday, I think maybe I'll be a teacher and listen to the stories of my students.

8 Who Needs a Storyteller for Freshman Comp?

Sharon Kane

September 8
Dear Journal,

I'm starting you for one reason—you're a class assignment! I've never kept a diary, I've always thought they were stupid, and I hate to write—so there! I haven't the faintest idea of what I'm supposed to be doing. My writing teacher, Ms. Spencer, says we don't *have* to have any ideas—if we "freewrite," as she calls it, something will happen. I'll believe it when I see it. She says that we're supposed to write whatever comes into our heads, and that we can't let the pencil stop—even if we have to write the same sentence over and over.

Since nothing is coming into my head and my required writing time isn't up, I'll describe my first class, *her* class, which was not what I pictured my first college class would be like. I was prepared for hard work: I was prepared for a scholarly lecture. Instead what we got was stories!!! As she was calling the roll, she kept telling us about her family. I think I must know half the Spencers ever born. When she got down the class list to a guy named Joe (a cute guy, by the way), she told him she was doing research on Josephs and asked him if he had ever fallen out of anything. He said yes, a chairlift, which made us all laugh (I guess everyone was as nervous as I was at first) and she proceeded to tell us about all the things her son Joseph had fallen out of—his highchair, a tree, the family truck.

As she responded to other people introducing themselves, we learned about her other son (an upcoming Michael J. Fox, she says), her daughter, her husband, her sisters, one of whom has been in college for eight and a half years, changing her major—makes me wonder how many times I'll change mine before I know what I want to be—her aunt Grace, and her mother-in-law (who sounds like quite a character). Uh-oh, I was afraid I'd have nothing to write, and I have now gone over my time limit *and* written a run-on sentence! I never thought I'd get to know a college professor so well, especially not on the first day of class! However, I'm really nervous about college writing and I don't want her to use too much of our time fooling around. I need her to *teach* me writing. I'm scared to death about what to write about. I can never think of a topic. I wonder if she assigns topics?

September 18
Dear Journal,

Our teacher is nuts. Halfway through class today, Ms. Spencer stopped mid-sentence and said, "Did I tell you my mother-in-law is coming in thirty-one days and three hours?" She went on to regale us with memories of past holidays with "Grandma S." We were practically on the floor, and she told the stories so vividly that I can still picture her mother-in-law standing by the Christmas tree, criticizing the placement of the tinsel, then reaching up to fix Joey's mistake and falling into the tree, toppling everything over.

I've found out that Ms. Spencer doesn't confine her stories to her own family. Every Friday as we leave for the weekend she warns us, "Don't smoke funny cigarettes; don't drink ugly stuff," and then tells us about some former student who didn't follow her advice—today's example joined the circus while under the influence. She has excellent attendance because we don't want to miss the fun!

Also, today we heard the story of *Gypsy Rose Lee.* Why, in a writing course, you ask? Well, Dear Journal, I'll tell you in my teacher's words. "As writers, your crucial paragraphs will be your first, where you wow them, and your last, where you leave 'em wanting more."

October 10
Dear Journal,

Today we had to come to class prepared to tell our favorite story. Ms. Spencer told us about her son Joey's favorite stories, the *Frog and Toad* series by Arnold Lobel. He met the author at his school. Mr. Lobel even "slapped him five," and now Joey goes to bed each night and listens to his Arnold Lobel tapes.

We had a great time hearing each other's favorite stories: Rapunzel, Curious George, Babar, Amelia Bedelia, Mrs. Piggle-Wiggle. But once again, I was asking myself how this was going to help us write. Well, Journal, it seems to have something to do with "adapting to audience," something that seems pretty important to our teacher. She told us to rewrite our stories so that her six-year-old Joseph could understand them. You know, I tried it tonight and it wasn't as easy as I thought it would be!

October 23
Dear Journal,

The title of today's entry is, "When is off-the-topic *not* off-the-topic?" Whenever Ms. Spencer comes into class, the first thing we hear about is how her morning went at home and what her kids are up to. We know when Chas forgets his cleats for soccer practice, when Joey has a science project due, when her husband eats the Froot Loops she had bought for a craft project. Today we heard about Carey arguing at the breakfast table trying to get her mother to buy her a new prom dress. She went into great detail. Now, you know me, Journal, I don't like time wasted, and, as usual, was wondering what this has to do with our writing class. Well, guess what? The daughter's whole logical argument turned out to be a model argumentative essay! It even had a concession paragraph, admitting that she did have another dress, and that money was tight, but then it went on to give supporting reasons for her "thesis." Can you imagine? It certainly lessened our fears about writing an argumentative essay—we speak them every day!

November 2
Dear Journal,

Ms. Spencer often tells stories of her childhood in Zag, Kentucky. Today she had us practically able to feel the coolness of the water when she described swimming with her family in the river on hot nights. Her voice was almost a whisper as she described herself curled up in a tree in a cow pasture, listening to her parents call her name. While she had us entranced, she said in a sort of hypnotic tone, "Now write a description of a place that stands out in your memory of your childhood." We all wrote silently, like we were still feeling the magic and then creating our own magic. It wasn't until tonight that I realized I didn't freeze like I usually do when teachers give an assignment. She modeled a description for us, and provided an example that showed us what she meant but didn't confine us. Maybe I'm not such a dunce when it comes to writing after all!

November 15
Dear Journal,

Another childhood story today. When she was four, Ms. Spencer watched a kitten being born. It was ugly and wet and dirty. But when the mother cleaned it up it got better looking, and later in the day it got still better looking, and in a few more days it was running around and it was fluffy and pretty and alive and complete. She tells us that's what the writing process (one of her favorite phrases) is like. "It starts out messy and yucky, but it keeps being revised until it's something beautiful." Tonight's assignment is to reflect on our personal writing process. We can take any piece of writing we've done, whether it's an academic paper or a love poem, and tell the story of its creation, its birth. I never thought much about how I wrote. Much as I hate to admit it, Dear Journal, this could be fun! Bye!!

November 26
Dear Journal,

Today we were entertained with stories of the Spencer Family Reunion. We were introduced to Uncle Bolger, the family drunk, Aunt May, the family floozie, Boo, the family nut, etc., etc. Ms. Spencer says she plays the role of the family mentor; everyone comes to her for advice. (Between you and me, Journal, I'll bet she also plays the role of the family storyteller. She has a story for everything!) Just as we had settled into a nice listening mode, ready to be entertained for the whole period, Ms. Spencer said, "Now fill in this blank: "My role in the family is that of . . ." After a few minutes of silence, we began to talk about what we had written. Alice said she was the family pet. Ken said he was the family fixer. I realized I was the family dreamer. We were anxious to tell our stories and hear about each other. It was easy to do because of the family reunion story Ms. Spencer had started us off with. There was lots of talk. Our assignment for tonight—you guessed it—write about our role in the family. I think all our talk today served as a kind of prewriting, so I'm going to start my first draft now. Later!

December 4
Dear Journal,

You can tell that Ms. Spencer is preoccupied with her daughter's prom night. We were working in peer groups today, responding to each other's drafts, and several people had teacher conferences. I overheard Ms. Spencer talking to someone about her draft. "It's as if you think you're all ready for your date; you've got your earrings on, and shoes and underwear—but no dress. This here is just not enough to get you to the prom, dear." The writer laughed and shook her head. I thought to myself, "That's neat. That's so much better than getting a paper back with 'No substance' or 'Needs further development' scrawled in the margin." Ms. Spencer's stories strike again!

December 14
Dear Journal,

Wait till you hear what happened tonight! I was at a frat party, and I met a guy—a senior. We were making small talk, you know, introductory kind of conversation, and he asked me who I had for Freshman Comp. When I said Ms. Spencer, he yelled out, "How's her mother-in-law?" I cracked up, but really, it's got me thinking. Here's a teacher who left an impression, who is remembered by students. He told me, "She believed in us. She cared so much about us, and we were so close to her, that we figured we couldn't give her anything but our very best work." Wow! Did her stories do that? That's powerful!

December 21
Dear Journal,

Here we are at the end of the semester. I feel so different from when I first started giving my thoughts and complaints to you. For one thing, I know now that you've become my friend as well as my first audience (Ms. Spencer told us audience was important!).

Guess it's time to answer the question that serves as the title of this journal. Who needs a storyteller for Freshman Comp? *I* do, although I did not realize it for a while. I have come to appreciate all that Ms. Spencer's stories did for our class. They established an immediate and strong rapport with the teacher. Our collective laughter at Ms. Spencer's outrageous family tales bound us together and helped establish a community feeling, which we needed as we worked collaboratively and responded to each other's drafts in peer response groups. Ms. Spencer built a base of information by her storytelling which she then drew from when she needed to make a point about writing in general or about a particular piece of student writing.

Most important of all, Ms. Spencer helped us to learn that we all had stories to tell, and could tell them effectively in writing. I am a storyteller. Want proof, Dear Journal? *You* are the proof. I have written the story of my first semester in a college class. And the main character has been a dynamic one, growing and learning more about herself. I can't wait until next semester, when I will live another story, write another chapter. Thank you, Ms. Spencer, for stories.

9 Andrew Joins the Storytelling Club

Barbara A. Connelly

Storytelling in my middle school classes overflowed into an afternoon "club," which one sixth grader refers to as "our family." We are a family in many ways, sharing our little stories, real and fictional, and yet we are different from each other as only fifth graders can be from eighth graders. We are certainly an international family. We could have our own Tower of Babel if all the first languages surfaced. We swing from Vietnam through Kansas to Mexico for our roots, and our ages range from ten to a very old fourteen. The personalities range from a lively cheerleader to a noticeably withdrawn Andrew.

Andrew, like some others, came, listened, and seemed to enjoy, but hesitated to participate. I had only known Andrew from a fifth-grade speech and drama class I had taught for a mere nine weeks. There had been thirty-six in the class, and I had just barely remembered Andrew telling an Aesop fable and making it interesting.

Then one day in storytelling club, Andrew volunteered to tell a story. The other children looked at him as though he were new. They had allowed him to become invisible. Despite our relaxed format, I was nervous for Andrew. I so desperately wanted him to be accepted and feel encouraged to participate more. With downcast head, Andrew squirmed onto the storytelling stool, wrapped his legs around its legs, lifted his eyes, and began. It was a tall tale and Andrew told it with a slight twang. Slowly, he worked his way through the fifteen-minute story, down to the surprise ending. When he looked around at the finish, only silent stares met his eyes. We were still recovering from his spell. At last, we started clapping and congratulating him. His eyes sparkled and a slight smile appeared, then disappeared, as he went to his seat and became invisible again behind a passive face and hooded eyes.

Later, when I praised Andrew's efforts to his homeroom teacher, she was amazed. He was a dilemma in her class. Despite very high test scores, he never participated or did his work. His handwriting was illegible and his voice could barely be heard, even when he did speak. He was receiving extra help outside the classroom and was seeing a counselor because of severe home problems. He was a social loner and considered "at risk."

At the next storytelling meeting, someone asked Andrew where he heard the story he had told, and he replied that it was on a tape owned by a friend of his mother. The tape was *The Checker-Playing Hound Dog* and had many tall tales on it. Andrew then proceeded to share another one. It was equally as long as the first, and once again Andrew developed a twang. His stories were longer and more involved than any that the others had tried, and I could feel that the students were popping with more questions for him, about the twang, how many times had he heard the tape, etc. But they sensed that Andrew was not yet ready to risk opening up to us, and it was a common feeling that we should wait until he was ready. Andrew remained the same at our meetings, only becoming visible when he "told." I saw him often in the office; he seemed to be getting a lot of detentions, but he never acknowledged my presence, and we kept our friendship a secret.

Later in the year, I was judging acts for a talent show, when the door opened and the next presenter turned out to be Andrew. He handed in his vita with a closed look, and I gave him an eye hug for encouragement. Andrew's demeanor was in stark contrast to the vibrations left from previous tryouts. We had just finished six "lip acts" that had left their mark on our ears, but now, suddenly the room was too quiet. Everything seemed in slow motion; I felt that the air had even stopped circulating. The judges' eyes followed Andrew as he slowly curled his legs around the chair, wet his lips and began, "I remember when I was young . . ." The twang tied us to the story and the teller. Andrew's Will Rogers laid-back approach was mesmerizing. Despite his apparent nervousness, I could feel Andrew's confidence that he "had" us, right to the rib-tickling ending. Then, he gave us back to reality and he returned to his world. It was as if we had swapped places in a science fiction experiment.

He scored well enough to be included on the program, and when I told him the news, he looked frightened. He said that he didn't think he would be able to perform in front of the big kids and that maybe his stuttering would return. (I mentally gasped at this, as I had no idea that he was a stutterer.) I tried to encourage him, but later, when he didn't appear for the dress rehearsal, I told myself that perhaps it was too much for a fifth grader to take on not only adult audiences, but peers. I intended to praise him for trying when next I saw him, but before I could, he told me that his mother's car had broken down on the way to the dress rehearsal and he had a note for me, but he lost it.

The next evening, when his name was announced on stage, I held my breath. I looked up to see him winding around the chair legs, taking a deep breath, licking his lips, and in what seemed like an hour later, his twang began, and he was off. The audience seemed to be leaning forward to catch his every word and before long . . . "Just like I've been a-lyin' to you" brought us to reality and laughter and applause. Andrew uncoiled himself, bowed, almost smiled, and disappeared from view.

Our storytelling family engulfed Andrew after the program, claiming him as one of us. He almost said something, but caught himself. He didn't quite hold back the look that came into his eyes, however, that "Once upon a time" look, that "They lived happily ever after" look, the look of those who share the joys and the hopes found in storytelling.

As a teacher, I yearn for Andrew to be all he can be. As a friend, I want to spare him from his quiet desperations. As a fellow storyteller, I rejoice that perhaps he has found somewhere to "hang his hat," to attach his hopes, until he is ready to live happily ever after.

10 Edmund's Story

Mary Murphy

The New York State Division for Youth project proposal read: "Participating in the Storytelling Project will be a targeted group of Division for Youth residents who are educationally disadvantaged, are members of ethnic and minority groups in need of services and are confined to institutions. Residents will be introduced to the 'World's Oldest Art Form.' We hope the project will build their self-esteem by recognizing that their own stories are a part of a continuing tradition and by promoting problem-solving through creation of stories, songs and dramatization."

I was hired last fall as part of this project—introducing storytelling to two workshop groups of ten boys each at Parker Center in Redhook, New York. One of the groups was made up of kids who were so "educationally disadvantaged" that they could barely read or write. Some had learning disabilities; some had physical disabilities; all were sentenced to Parker by a judge for having committed a crime. They were a captive audience. And as it turned out, all of them loved storytelling. They found out right away that they were good at it—completely natural at imagining and performing stories. For some of them, it was probably the first thing they were good at in school, and that's all they needed to know. We spent our time together creating our own stories: building them up bit by bit, acting them out, trying different endings, and finally recording them. Writing them down seemed out of the question. Nobody knew much about writing. But telling was definitely in. And when they saw that I was really listening, it was, for them, a sweet and cherished form of self expression.

On Friday at the end of our first week, we sat in a circle and told stories. I told one, and then Albert told about a nearsighted turtle named Bart. Angel had one about a boy named Jerry who went fishing with his father and caught tons of fish, and James had a pet snake— a python—who got run over by a steamroller.

We had been going on for quite a while when Edmund raised his hand. He had never done that before and I was surprised. Edmund only had one hand that he could use; his left hand was badly deformed. It looked like a crab's pincers with only a thumb and index finger.

Whenever he had to speak to an adult, he automatically hid it behind his back. He had done his best to resemble a piece of furniture all week, and I was amazed to see him wanting my attention.

Edmund was fourteen, quiet and watchful. He had the reserved dignity of a born leader. The other boys respected him but kept their distance. He sat in the back of the room, often with his eyes closed, sometimes obviously asleep. When I would ask him a question, he would consider it carefully, reply politely, and withdraw again into his well-protected space. Although I couldn't really say why, I liked him and I was glad to have him in the workshop.

Edmund told us, in his quiet voice, that he had made up a story, even written part of it down the night before. He had a single scrawled-upon folded-up piece of paper in his good hand, and we all waited while he flattened it out against his leg. He began by reading from the paper, but soon ran out of written words and continued on his own. This is Edmund's story:

> Out on the streets there was a boy named Rap who was 14 and a very successful drug dealer. Came to school wearing a $200.00 bomber jacket, designer jeans, gold chains. He carried a wad of bills in his pockets. He was a mean boy. Nobody got in his way. The principal at his school asked him "Are you dealing drugs?" and Rap said, "I'm not telling you." He just smiled and left the building.
>
> Rap had little kids doing his running for him. They delivered the drugs and brought him the money. Rap had a gun he carried so that if anything went wrong with the deal he had protection from his supplier. He used little kids to run for him because you don't need bail to get them out of jail. The Mother can get them out.
>
> One of Rap's boys was a ten year old kid named Anthony. Anthony's mother was on crack and Anthony worked for Rap to get his Mother her drug. One day Anthony's little sister ate one of the crack capsules off the living room carpet. She got herself a drink of water and started spitting up white and red blood. Then she just fell over and died.
>
> One day Rap was waiting in the alley for Anthony to bring him the cash from a deal. But something went wrong because Anthony was late and when he came he didn't have the money. Rap thought Anthony's mother took the money off him. Anthony was crying telling Rap that the men had taken the drugs and beat him up. Rap was mad. He didn't believe Anthony so he pulled out his gun, put it to Anthony's head, and pulled the trigger. Rap got out of there fast but later the police came looking for him. Rap tried to shoot the cop but the cop shot

him in the leg. They arrested him and the judge sent him upstate to do his time.

Everyone was quiet after Edmund told his story. He had told it so compellingly and with such conviction that, although he had barely raised his voice above a whisper, he had held us all spellbound. I figured at least part of it must have been true. Anthony may have been his cousin or some neighborhood friend.

I was about to comment on what good storytelling it was when one of the other kids, Chris, suddenly turned to Edmund and said "Word up, Man." Then someone else said "Word up, Man," and pretty soon everyone in the room was looking at Edmund and saying "Word up, Word up." I had heard them say it before when expressing agreement with a speaker. Like people exclaiming Amen! in church. Then Chris turned to me and said, "Rap's his name, Miss Murphy. That story's about him. That's how he got sent to Parker."

I stared at Chris, hardly able to understand what he was saying. Edmund was the dealer? Edmund was Rap? Edmund put a gun to a ten-year-old boy's head and shot him? I looked at Edmund, waiting for him to deny it, to tell Chris he was a liar, but he didn't move; but just looked down at the desk and didn't look up again for a long time.

I felt as if I was going to be sick. I knew they had all done things against the law, but I thought it was stuff like shoplifting or writing graffiti on subway cars or running away from home. We had been having such fun telling stories to each other. But Edmund was a murderer and I was the only naïve jerk who didn't know it. I felt as if I'd been lied to.

The session was almost over, and I was trying hard to control my voice as I gave out assignments for next week. When the bell rang, the boys pulled their books together and ran out, telling me they'd see me next week and to bring more stories.

Soon they were all gone except Edmund, who still sat looking down at his desk. After a few minutes, he walked over to where I was pretending to be busy, shoving books and papers into my bag. I couldn't look at him. He said, "Are you mad at me because of my story?" I thought of Anthony with a gun touching his head, Edmund standing over him, how scared he must have been. "Are you mad at me because of my story?" Edmund said again. I opened my mouth to say something but started to cry instead. I didn't know I was going to do that but I couldn't help it. I stood there crying and Edmund stood there watching me, still waiting for an answer, I guess. When I pulled myself together I said, "No, Edmund, I'm not mad at you." Then he said, "Can I come back to the storytelling next week?"

I looked at Edmund—educationally disadvantaged member of a minority group in need of services—drug dealer, corrupter of young children, coldblooded killer. Desperately trying to hide his grotesquely shaped hand behind his back, actually holding it behind him with his good hand. And I said, "Yes, Edmund, you can come back next week. See you Monday." He nodded then and left the room.

A few weeks after I had finished at Parker, I got a bunch of "thank you for coming" letters from the boys sent by their English teacher. Among them was one from Edmund. It said:

Dear Ms. Murphy,

I wanted to say thank you for coming up and taking your time for coming up here at Eddie A. Parker and reading—or—telling us stories. I must say the stories you told was really excellent. Even though I felt asleep. But when I was—or—I did stay awake, your stories sound great. You know I wanted to say something to you. Telling stories is a gift. There aren't that many people out their who could tell stories like you. You are a lucky person. You are a good person. Good things come to good people.

Yours truly,
Edmund J. Austin

11 Telling the Tale

Syd Lieberman

After the bell, Hilary came up to my desk. "Mr. Lieberman," she asked, "can I write about the death of a friend's brother? He died of cystic fibrosis in eighth grade. I knew him really well."

My high school students always have the option to write about personal subjects. In fact, all my writing assignments have choices that encourage them to apply the themes of the literature we are reading to their own lives.

I think this is one way for students to deal with the problems of growing up. Then, too, I believe that students learn how to write only when they *want* to write, when they really want to tell you something. I could see that Hilary was about to deal with an important issue in her life.

But when the paper came in, it was flat. The facts were present, but there was a detached quality to the writing. It felt as if I had assigned the topic, as if she were a prisoner fulfilling a requirement for parole. I knew she hadn't done what she wanted to do, and I knew there was a story there that hadn't reached the paper.

We all have received papers like this one, papers where the real story is still in the writer's head. I decided to use a simple storytelling device to help Hilary get to the heart of the experience: I just get a student up in front of the class and have him or her tell the story. Afterward, the class asks questions of the student about any moment or scene that they want more information about or that confused them.

When students have the opportunity to develop the story orally in a conversational situation, they feel comfortable because the situation is so familiar. Often the story begins to flow. It always amazes me to see how many important details a student leaves out of a paper.

I privately asked Hilary if I could get her up in front of the class to do this exercise. She quickly agreed, saying that many of the students knew the boy in her story and that she wouldn't feel uncomfortable talking about him. Because of the nature of the subject, I decided to be the one to ask her questions.

Before the class came in, I listed all the anecdotes Hilary had included in her paper. All I did was ask her to tell me more about each one.

Nothing special was happening, and I was just about to let the situation pass. After all, David had died just three years earlier. Perhaps Hilary was still too close to it to really look at it.

Then we came to a one-line paragraph which occurred late in the paper. Hilary had written, "And who could forget the time David scored a basket in the basketball game?" That was it.

I said, "Hilary, now tell us about the basketball game."

And she said, "Oh, it was so wonderful. He loved basketball but he was too sick to really play. He used to dress for the games and sit at the end of the bench and cheer. They would always put him in with a minute or so to go, just so he could feel like part of the team.

"And then, in the last game of the season, when they put him in, the ball came to him for the first time all year. And he took it and threw it up just as the buzzer sounded. And the ball went in. And we all started to yell, 'David, David, David.' And we rushed out of the stands and picked him up and carried him off on our shoulders."

I'll never forget the moment when she finished. She was crying. I was crying. Kids in the class were crying. Hilary had found her story.

I told her that whatever she did in revision, that scene was the heart of the piece. She turned in a powerful piece of writing. David had died a few months after this moment on the basketball court, and Hilary went straight from the basketball triumph to the funeral. It was a moving tribute to her friend's brother.

Hilary became a storyteller in this assignment. It's what I want all my students to experience sometime during my class. For some, it's easy. They feel comfortable on paper. They have easy access to their imaginations and their memories.

But for others, it is a difficult task. There are many ways to help. But getting students to tell their stories out loud allows many to discover just what it is they want to say. Making students storytellers can help them become writers.

12 Family Stories, Images, and the Fictional Dream

Tom Romano

Late one evening my daughter, Mariana, stepped into the room where I sat before the computer. She was eighteen then, in the last month of her senior year of high school.

"Will you listen to my story?" she asked.

Closing in on some writing of my own, I turned my head to her but kept my fingers at the keyboard. Mariana wore sweats. Her blond hair was clipped back from her forehead. Her contact lenses were soaking in a heat sterilizer for the night. Her glasses had slid halfway down her nose; she pushed them into place with a forefinger. She looked weary. Track practice had been longer than usual. In her hand she held a dozen sheets of ragged-edged notebook paper she liked to write on with soft-leaded pencils. I knew those pages were the draft of her final paper for senior English. She had been thinking about this assignment for months, researching here and there, gathering information and impressions, asking me questions about my family. Since her late supper of microwaved leftovers, she had been in her room, bent over her desk, filling pages with her looping handwriting.

For this assignment Mariana's teacher had asked the students to research particular years or eras and then—instead of composing traditional research papers—to write short fiction that incorporated details from their research. Mariana had made the assignment her own, had chosen to research Ellis Island and 1914, the year my father, then a boy of nine, emigrated to the United States from Italy.

Mariana dropped to the floor and sat cross-legged to read me her story. I removed my fingers from the keyboard and swiveled around to face her. She read, turning the pages sideways at times to read words written in the margins, looking closely other times to make out words she had squeezed between lines.

Slightly different versions of this essay were published as the epilogue to the author's dissertation (University of New Hampshire) and in *English Journal* 82 (September 1993), 34–36.

"Felice felt he was drowning in the ocean of people," she read. "He closed his eyes and tried to breathe. He could feel the small wooden pony against his heart and remembered Luca. Tears welled in his eyes but he swallowed them this time. Giuesseppe would call him *bambino* again and hit him. Felice wanted to be strong too, and he wanted to be able to stand up to Papa like Giuesseppe said he was going to."

Elbows on my knees, chin resting in my hands, I gazed down at my daughter, then let my eyelids close. I entered the fictional dream Mariana had woven of my father, his two brothers, sister, and mother as they shuffled along in a crowd, moving off the ship that had brought them across the Atlantic Ocean. Filomena, the youngest child, slept in her mother's arms. Antonio, the youngest boy, cried and held his mother's skirt. Giuesseppe, the oldest child, carried himself bravely, almost disdainfully, as he moved toward American soil. Felice, my father, was between his brothers, but closer to Antonio's tears than Giuesseppe's defiance. The wooden pony Felice kept in his shirt pocket had been carved and given to him by his friend, Luca, before the family left the village near Naples.

In her short story, Mariana explored a mystery she had been aware of for years—the great influence on our lives of my father, dead then twenty-five years, the mythlike story of his family's immigration to an America decades away from fast-food restaurants, designer jeans, and alternative rock music. She conjectured in her fiction, too, inventing detail, action, and characterizations that have not been documented in family stories, but that carry the illusion of reality, nevertheless.

Mariana's research in books had not been extensive. A half dozen times, however, she had watched the opening of Francis Ford Coppola's *The Godfather II*, the scenes when the Italian immigrants enter New York harbor, are awestruck by the Statue of Liberty, and disembark at Ellis Island. These images had shown Mariana early twentieth century America and the look of frightened, hopeful immigrants. The images spurred her imagination, bringing new vividness to the stories told and retold by members of our family, stories I had heard my father and aunts and uncles tell when I was a boy sitting at the dining room table after a traditional Christmas Eve supper, stories that rolled from their tongues in the quiet fullness after the meal, stories that sparked further stories and drew my beloved relatives into debates about events, people, and memories.

During those fleeting hours of storytelling, I sat transfixed, asking questions that prompted an uncle or aunt to retell some incident or maybe, just maybe, reveal some bit of information I had never heard before. And when my uncles and aunts and father slipped into the assured rhythms of reminiscence, I hoped that the telephone would not ring and that no one would knock at the door. Carefully, quietly, I refilled the small glasses with the dry red wine my uncle made each year. I wanted nothing—not an empty glass, not an unexpected call, not a glance at the clock—to break the spell of telling.

Mariana leaned forward, reading slowly, treating her language with great respect, adopting a colloquial tone when she read dialogue. Her sincere, urgent voice rolled up to me from the floor and entered my very bones. I had never imagined my father as a boy at the moment he arrived in America, never imagined that he may have left a best friend in Italy, that his sister may have slept and younger brother may have cried. Because of "The Wooden Pony," Mariana's fictional dream woven of image and story, language and imagination, I would never think of my father in the same way again. Mariana read the final lines:

> Felice looked past Mama and met the gaze of Giuesseppe. He watched two tears roll out of his older brother's eyes and make their varied path down his face.
> The two brothers stared at each other, expressionless. Felice grinned. *"Bambino,"* he whispered.
> They laughed silently together. Felice patted his heart and thought about the future.

Mariana looked up to me and saw my eyes filled with tears.

A day or two after that evening I thought of buying Mariana a carved wooden pony for her high school graduation. I had no luck finding such a present in area stores. I remained optimistic, though, since I was traveling a good deal. On trips to Calgary, Toronto, Montana, and New York, I found wooden bears, raccoons, wolves, seals, whales, moose, but no wooden ponies. Not even wooden horses.

My mother-in-law saved the day. She knew a wood carver, a longtime friend, who agreed to whittle a wooden pony for me. I sent him a copy of Mariana's short story so that he could generate his own vision. Before he began his wood working, however, he suffered a heart attack and underwent triple-bypass surgery.

Two months later I learned that he still wanted to carve the pony, that he and his wife, in fact, thought the work would be good therapy for him. By this time it was mid-summer.

"Are you getting me something for graduation or not?" Mariana asked.

"Be patient," I told her.

The following year, ten months after she had written "The Wooden Pony," Mariana was home from college for spring break. The day before she headed back to school, she and her mother went shopping. When they were gone, a small package arrived in the mail. I opened it and pulled out an object wrapped in tissue paper: a stiff-legged, blockish wooden pony. I turned it over in my hands, touching the ears, running my finger along the smooth back. I stood the pony on the kitchen counter. I was disappointed; it looked amateurish.

I found a note from the wood carver's wife. "Merle wasn't happy with the way this turned out," she wrote, "but our ten-year-old grandson loves it and wanted to take it home. We thought it might be just the thing Luca would have carved for Felice."

Precisely, I thought.

Mariana arrived home from shopping in a flurry, dropping plastic bags to the floor and plopping down to open them. I sat reading in a chair.

"Open the package on the counter," I said to her.

Mariana was busy removing skirt, sweater, and shoes from the bags.

"What's in it?" She laid the sweater against the skirt on the floor and eyed the combination.

"Just open it. Please."

"I will in a minute," she said, her voice colored with annoyance. She spent a moment or two more with her new clothes, then walked to the refrigerator and opened a can of soda pop. Finally, she turned to the package. Her eyebrows were pursed, troubled, as I had often seen my father's. From the package Mariana lifted the object. The tissue paper fell away. She held the wooden pony in both hands, her eyebrows raised in startled surprise. She glanced across the room to me. And this time, this time it was her eyes that filled with tears.

Mariana's fictional dream had taken me to a place I had never been, enabled me to imagine my father as a boy wearing a coarse, woolen cap and high-topped, black leather shoes. The story went far beyond the classroom, much farther than the teacher could have imagined. Mariana's uncles, aunts, and cousins, great-uncles, great-aunts, and grandmother read the story and talked about it and read it again. The story triggered further stories.

Mariana's story reached back seventy-five years, to a moment when an immigrant child stepped ashore at Ellis Island. America and his life lay before him. And years later, one of his granddaughters, a girl born seven years after his death, thought long about this grand-father she knew only through family stories and photographs, wondered further about a magical day in October 1914 that her relatives had talked about ever since she could remember. Powerful images took shape and language stirred. Setting became real. Characters spoke and moved. Mariana wrote a fictional dream. And we who entered that dream were never the same.

13 Telling Tales from School

Barbara Lipke

I suppose I have always told stories, just like everybody else, but I became a storyteller gradually. It was a metamorphosis, a change that seemed to take place as naturally and inevitably as the journey of larva to butterfly.

My first classroom storytelling came about in the late sixties. I was trying to teach my students how to build suspense and I told them about a ghost that invaded my house one moonless midnight. At the climax of my demonstration I yelled, "Who's there?"

The connecting door to my teaching partner's room burst open.

"What's wrong?" he demanded looking wildly about the silent room.

"Nothing," I said. "I'm just telling a story."

"What?" He looked confused and retreated into his room, closing the door behind him.

The students were impatient. "What happened?" they demanded. I was distracted by the interruption. They were not. It was my first hint of the power of storytelling.

I did not think of myself as a storyteller then or for many years after that. In fact, I did not know that such a thing existed in our twentieth century world. In 1976 I returned from a sabbatical leave to a difficult class of sixth graders. One day my teaching partner said, "Jay O'Callahan's coming tomorrow."

"What's that?" I asked.

"He's a storyteller."

"How long do we have to keep the kids quiet?"

"No. No, it's not like that," he said.

The next day we had fifty-five sixth graders sitting on the floor. The door opened and in came a tall, gangly man with a large Adam's apple, wearing a red and white polo shirt and green chinos.

"Forget it," I thought.

For the next hour no one stirred. During one of O'Callahan's stories, the students stared at the steam pipe in the corner of the ceiling and saw firelight dancing on a fluted marble column. I did too. I began to see the power of storytelling.

I was hooked. I decided to take storytelling seriously. By 1983 I was telling stories professionally and had begun to teach my students to be storytellers. At the request of colleagues, I began to write a storytelling teaching unit.

There are many reasons for telling stories—and many stories that can illustrate each reason. I tell stories to entertain, to teach, to build a community of sharing. I teach students to be storytellers to build their self-esteem, to give them new skills, and to enhance skills they already have. Sharing stories helps them understand themselves and each other. Storytelling can be a key to understanding the other person's values, the values of different cultures and beliefs. The following stories of storytelling are brief glances into those worlds.

In 1986 I went to China with a group of high school students; several of them had been in my sixth-grade class. In China, we stayed in university dormitories and took long train rides. Twenty-four hours was standard. The trains moved slowly so we saw a lot of the countryside, but that's another story. Four adults shared a cramped compartment, but often twenty or more students would pack themselves into the narrow space, sit on the bunks, the floor, press in from the corridor, and demand stories.

Once, as I finished a story, a young man who had been in my class five years earlier spoke up accusingly:

"You changed it!"

"I did?"

"Yes, when you told it before. . . ." He went on to point out details of the story that had changed over my years of telling it.

"Is it better or worse?" I asked him.

"It's different. It should be the same!"

I had disturbed an important memory and disturbed it with a change of details so small I did not remember what they were, but Bill remembered!

Another year I had a split grade (4/5) and in the course of the year told a couple of short Native American tales, one in the fall and one in the spring. The following year, having kept most of my fourth graders as fifths, I showed a wonderful Canadian film called *The Loon's Necklace*. It is a depiction, with traditional masks, of a Native American myth. When the film was over, I asked the class about "common elements" they found in the film—expecting them to list the forces of nature, storms, wind, the four directions. What they identified, however, were details they remembered from the stories I had told more than a year earlier, elements that were also found in the myth of "The Loon's Necklace." They remembered that birds dove to the bottom of the water, that there were birds and animals in all three stories; and they remembered which ones belonged in each story. The details came flooding back; they could re-create each story even though they had heard those stories only once. It occurred to me then, and I still believe, that storytelling imprints and affects memory as no other kind of teaching does.

As my own storytelling expanded, along with my uses of storytelling in the classroom, I found that in the hands of my students it became a powerful teaching and learning tool. One year, I offered storytelling as a way for students to present research they had done in social studies. Fifth graders were presenting their social studies projects on the Civil War.

The class had been busily taking notes on Robert E. Lee, the battles of Bull Run, the Missouri Compromise.

"What was that date?"

"Not so fast. Which side was the *Merrimac* on?"

"So we have to know all the states that seceded?"

The students were all at sea. There didn't seem to be any sense of the whole—only the parts. No cause and effect relationships. I worried. What would these ten-year-olds get out of their two-month-long unit on the Civil War?

Then Kathy stood up to present her research on the Ku Klux Klan. She had decided to create and tell a historical fiction story as her project. But as she stood before the class, her confidence failed.

"Don't take out your pencils. There's no information in this story. In fact, I don't even know why I'm standing here taking your time," Kathy apologized. But as she began to tell her story, her apologetic manner disappeared. As we watched, Kathy *became* a freed black man after 1878, determined that his children would learn to read and write, no matter what the cost. In the story, (s)he crept into the white school, night after night to copy the lessons left on the blackboard onto scraps of paper by moonlight or a flickering candle. He was seen and the knights of the KKK burned his crops. He went back, although his wife and children begged him not to, and the KKK rode again. I glanced quickly around my classroom. Twenty-four students listened, glued in place. They were present with Kathy, with the character she had become, on that hot, humid night, watching, hearing, smelling, feeling as the house was burned and the man's son shot.

Afterwards, there was silence: a tribute to the tale and the teller. And then, slowly, like an awakening, exclamations, talk, and applause. Not the polite, required applause that fifth graders give any project, but amazed, sustained applause. Kathy was stunned by the response.

Later, with the end-of-unit test, there was further evidence of the effectiveness of the story: more than 90 percent of the class chose to write about the Ku Klux Klan, and all of them understood the how, the why, and the effect, short term and long, of that terrorist organization. Those students, if they took nothing more from their two-month study, would never forget the KKK and how it affected post-Reconstruction history.

When I shared the results of her storytelling with Kathy, she was astounded.

"Me? I did that?"

The teaching unit grew each year. The fifth grade did an immigration unit as part of their American history social studies. I required that each student research and write her or his own anecdotal family history. That year, I had an Israeli student, Irit, an extremely shy and frightened little girl.

On her first day of school she came with her parents and the school guidance counselor. She moved absolutely silently into the classroom and to her desk. The fact that there were other Israeli children didn't seem to help. She sat silent and wide-eyed all day and fled as the bell rang at the end of the day.

Each day Irit appeared on time. She struggled with her work and was as shy, I learned, with the Hebrew bilingual teacher as she was with us. The students, especially her compatriots, tried to make her comfortable but to no avail.

Irit's understanding of English improved, and it was clear she understood a great deal of what went on. One day I told a story. I could see her concentrating on every word, fully engaged in the story. Another day I told her that her entrance ticket to the classroom was one sentence (a different one each day) spoken to me as she came into the room. The sentence was often so quiet, so barely breathed, that I had trouble hearing it. Little by little she began to take part in the class.

One day I announced to the class that we were about to start on storytelling, that as part of their family history research, each child was to find and tell an anecdote about someone in his or her family.

Irit seemed to shrink. Her brown eyes filled with tears and she ran from the classroom at the end of the day.

The next morning her sentence was, "Do I have to tell a story?"

"Yes, Irit. Of course. Everyone will tell a story."

"Can't I just write it?"

"I'll make it easy. It will be fun. You'll see."

The storytelling unit is a long one, full of story games, cooperative stories, and telling, telling, telling, first one with a rehearsal partner for specific response (as would occur in a writing conference), and then telling to a small group, and finally to the whole class. When Irit told her story to me, we sat knee to knee and she spoke so softly I could hardly hear her. The story was one about her mother as a little girl, and how she was blamed for something her brother had done. Irit told it in the first person, as her mother. Later, as she told it to a classmate, I saw her so involved in her story that she seemed to become her mother as a little girl. Finally she managed to tell it to the whole class. They broke into applause and cheers as she finished. She smiled and blushed, and thanked them.

The night we had all the families in for our Museum of Family History, it was Irit who asked if she could tell her story—to an audience of well over a hundred adults and children, most of them strangers to her. The power of storytelling had allowed the brave, self-confident Irit to emerge from the terrified little girl we had first met.

Each year, as my students begin work on their family stories, they sit in a circle on the floor and tell about their stories. It is only a sentence or two, but it gives them a chance to start sharing, and it also begins to weave the intercultural exchange that has become an important part of this unit.

"My story is about how my father escaped from the Holocaust," Jennifer said.

"What's that?" David asked.

I explained, but I too was startled. "Your father?" I asked. "Not your grandfather?"

"No. My father. At least that's what he told me."

"Okay," I said.

The story Jennifer told was, indeed, the story of her father's escape from the Holocaust when he was fourteen. He managed to escape from the factory, somewhere in eastern Europe, where he worked sixteen hours a day making boots for the German army; to slip, by night, past barbed wire fences, borders guarded by armed soldiers; to walk hundreds of miles and meet the liberating troops of the Allies. He ended up in Boston a year later, and at Harvard a year after that. When he and his wife came to our Museum of Family History, Jennifer's mother told me that her husband had never told that story before. She herself had not known it. Until Jennifer had interviewed him for her family history, he had never told anyone about his life before he came to Boston. The telling had made them all a closer family, she said. They were grateful for the opportunity to let the story do its healing work.

Storytelling expanded for me. As part of staff development, I began to work one day a week in other schools in the system, teaching students and teachers to be storytellers, spreading the word. I worked in many settings, prekindergarten to sixth grade, ESL, bilingual, and special education classes. George's story is one I remember well.

"Ahn Mo es sai, 'Yet my pe o ho!' " fifteen-year-old George struggled to say the words. His crutches supported him as he threw his arms wide in an effort to *be* Moses and to be sure that Pharaoh (and we) understood him.

George was a student in a special needs class. The students had a variety of needs and Tom's were the most severe: cleft palate, confined to crutches, developmentally delayed, with severe hearing and sight disabilities. Each day for this adolescent boy and his teacher was a struggle for communication and survival.

When I introduced storytelling to this class, I was unsure about whether it would work for them. They listened and enjoyed my stories—but how about theirs? I worked closely with their teacher, a remarkable woman. She taught me, as well as her students. The multiple handicapped twelve- to fifteen-year-olds had never performed at all, and storytelling is a sophisticated art. I wondered if it would prove too frustrating for them. Not at all, I learned. They were able to use storytelling in accordance with their own needs, and in spite of what I had seen to be serious limitations, George told the story of the Exodus. In spite of his speech problem, he told it with such passion that he saw the parting of the waters of the Red Sea and we did too.

Janise used her story as a way to work through her rejection by neighborhood peers, a problem she had not been able to articulate. Another child told a story about his family where unemployment and alcoholism were everyday facts.

Each student used storytelling differently. Some told traditional versions of "Little Red Riding Hood." Some retold the plots of television shows or movies. Yet for each student storytelling brought an opportunity to perform for an audience, to command attention in a legitimate way, even if only for a minute or two, for many of the stories were very brief. It was a first step, and when I left that classroom after my four once-a-week visits, the teacher and the students went eagerly on, using storytelling as an entrance to literature, as a way to enhance the children's listening and speaking skills, as vehicles for vocabulary development, and as a powerful builder of self-confidence.

It has been almost twenty years since Jay O'Callahan's storytelling hooked me. In this metamorphosis from larva to butterfly, I have told stories and encouraged students to tell stories in many different settings. I have learned that storytelling carries its own power—a power that sometimes has little to do with polished performance but that is evident in its effect on tellers and listeners alike.

III Coming Together: Building a Community of Listeners and Learners

Storytelling brings us together. Together we chuckle, we shiver, we wipe away tears. Together we learn to see everyday things in new ways—and to see not-so-everyday things in new ways. The stories in this section focus on how storytelling does bring us together, generating unique communities of learners and listeners.

"We found in Ithaca a community of fourteen-year-old story-tellers," says Anne Vilen. For her and the ninth graders in her first student-teaching experience, storytelling became the way to establish a sense of community: a community among themselves, a community with mythological heroes and heroines of the distant past, and a community with personal heroes and heroines of their own families. Anne relates how memories of her own father's stories impelled her to trust and value "the ever-changing story quilt of human history" that is stitched through a storytelling tradition.

Julia Hamilton finds that storytelling helps develop "first a community and then a community of learners" in her high school literature classes. She uses the oral telling of literary works as a way to heighten her students' awareness of their own processes in respond-ing to literature and to become aware of and to consider others' responses. Through the reflections and discussions that follow these retellings, her students' own ability to interpret literature is enhanced. As significantly, she finds that it is through the communal act of telling and hearing the stories that the students make deeper connections with themselves, with one another, and with their teacher.

Fifth-grade teacher Brian Conroy considers his elementary school to be an oasis in the middle of suburban San Jose, California, an oasis which is home to a community of students with widely different cultural and linguistic backgrounds. But it wasn't always that way; Brian confesses to having been stymied in finding the key that would open communication among his students. On the playground one day, he hit upon storytelling as a solution. Beginning with the development of their own "symbol language" and continuing with the use of various kinds of manipulatives, Brian and his class found that storytelling provided the breakthrough. From the students' excitement over storytelling grew an extensive folklore and storybook collection at his school: student-made books and audiotapes of folktales that students have told; collections of cross-cultural folklore, most of them recorded in both English and the native language; and a collection of storybooks in almost every language represented at the school.

In the final story, we see how teachers form a "folk culture," a unique "social community." Teachers in the same school share this community—as do teachers from different locales who have taught in different periods of time. What holds this community together is shared language, shared values and experiences, and shared stories. According to Bonnie Sunstein, as teachers "we need each other's stories in order to define our performances, understand our audiences, and most important, to inquire about and better understand what it is that we do."

As you give a listen to the stories in the final section of our book, we invite you to become a part of the exciting community of storytellers.

14 Story Quilt: A Student Teacher's Mythic Journey

Anne Vilen

I am piecing together stories, the family epic bequeathed to me by my father. Like patches of an old quilt, I trace them back to the original fabrics. This photo of Old Faithful erupting into the sunrise recalls a long drive through the predawn dark, me riding shotgun and listening to my father's exploits in Great Falls before the war. A remembered threshing rig silhouetted against the Big Sky sends me back to his mother managing the cook's car that trailed the wheat harvesters as they moved from farm to farm. I mend and stitch at a desk full of lesson notes, paper-clipped journals, books I mean to read again; my father's stories demand a place in this pedagogical canon. But they didn't always.

The first story called out to me one afternoon in the middle of a Greek mythology lesson I was giving to twenty-one ninth graders at a suburban southern school. I was a student teacher listening with unpracticed ears. These students would become my muse. But the muse would sing only after I had unlayered the ancient mythological quilt. Only after I had taught my students to read the meanings inscribed in its stitches. Only after we had learned together how to restore the text, how to match the color with stories from our own cultures, how to repair a broken seam with a thread of family history, how to darn a patch of new dream over a frayed edge. This ancient quilt, made whole by the preserving work of restoration and improvisation, is an inspiration to me now. I hear the muse laughing. She reminds me of that fateful day in class when I tripped over the story of Hercules strangling the snakes that Hera had sent to kill him. My father used to tell me this one all the time.

"Did I ever tell you about when I broke my leg? I was only five. Broke my leg sledding down the big hill across the railroad tracks from Grandma's. It was small-town Montana and the middle of the Depression, so I had to stay in the hospital three whole months in a cast from my hip to my toe. Yup, medicine wasn't so great then. One time they took the cast off so the doctor could x-ray my leg. They used a portable machine then that they rolled in on a cart, ya know, and set up next to the bed. A nurse was in the room with the doctor, and Mom of course. The nurse smeared some sticky stuff on my head and hooked some electrodes up to me. When the doctor pumped the button to shoot the x-ray—it was like, ya know, one of those squeeze triggers they have for cameras now—he accidentally bumped the x-ray machine against the metal part of my bed. The electric shock from that contact fizzled down the length of my body, went right through my big toe into the doctor, and laid him out dead right there on the cement floor. Knocked the nurse out cold and Mom too. Mom was the first one to come to. But I was okay. Burned all the hair off my head and burnt a hole a half inch across in my right big toe. You've seen the scar. I suppose that's why I went bald so early, on account of my hair had to start out twice."

My students leaned forward and their eyebrows rose. I heard a few incredulous NO WAYs from the back row. "Well, do you think Hercules really strangled those snakes when he was only a few months old? My father's story makes me and my family think of him as a survivor, a lucky man, blessed somehow. He endured an experience of passage. Hercules' story—and maybe the Greeks exaggerated theirs some too—was also a passage. It set the tone for his life of strength and heroism," I explained.

I had started my unit with a bag of generic implements scavenged in the course of teacher training—house rules about discipline and attendance, Madeline Hunter's eight-point lesson plan, a headful of pop psychology about how children learn. Having sought my teacher certification after seven years in another profession, I was more confident in the classroom than many student teachers. And for that reason I was given more rein by my cooperating teacher than the average newcomer. Still, I was concerned to be a professional teacher, not just an entertainer or buddy to my students. This story was a handcrafted invocation that caught me unawares. It wasn't supposed to come out in the middle of famed Edith Hamilton's scholarly discourse on the Greek classics. I felt ashamed when I first told it, was glad my cooperating teacher wasn't there to see me step out of my authoritative shoes and into mere conversation. I recovered quickly, locked the episode safely in the attic of memory, and proceeded down the primrose path of teaching.

But I kept running into thorns. A few weeks after that story, I gave a test on *The Odyssey.* After filling my grade book with *D*s and *F*s, I decided all those stories I had heard in the teachers' lounge about how students never do their reading or homework were true. Doubt crept in. I lay in bed angsting over poor explanations and conclusions interrupted by the clang of the bell. Guilt turned to penance. I spent the weekend writing individual comments on the students' exams, trying to prop up the spirits of those who fared the worst. On Monday I confessed to my adviser that *I* had failed the test—the test of my ability to teach in a way that compelled students to learn. She frowned at me worriedly and handed me an article on "how to manage." When she left I closed my classroom door and locked myself in. Shutting out the scornful stares of the central-office windows, which faced mine across a small courtyard, I hunkered down on the floor behind my desk and cried. As the sobs drummed through my trembling body, I wished myself back to that ragged, seven-times-upholstered chair where my father used to hold me in his lap and tell me stories. I pondered the learned doctor's electrocution and the child's good fortune, and I heard again the call of the muse.

When I arrived home, I rifled through my bankers' box of journals, starting with the first journal, assigned by my fifth-grade teacher, Ms. Wolfram: a lime green, twenty-nine-cent spiral notebook scribbled in blue pen with the words "my log," "private," "keepout," and "love" three times in bulging graffiti-style letters. I stopped at the one I had written in the ninth grade, a more sophisticated vinyl-bound calendar diary. In it I found an entry in which I described my teachers: the one who lowered our grades if we made wisecracks, the smart one who bored me to tears, the one who gave endless worksheets and graded primarily on spelling, and the one who asked us all to stand up and dance one day—Mr. Haebig. "Everyone stood up but nobody danced. Then Mr. Haebig said sit down if you feel uncomfortable. Everyone sat down. He showed us that *stress produces growth.* Through stress we learn to function in front of a group and live comfortably with stress." I wrote that as a student in the ninth grade. (I learned then, as now, through writing out my own experience.) But I didn't grasp the full meaning until I stepped into the shoes of my teacher; although the x-ray current of my father's story had also electrified my students, I had not listened to their response because being the storyteller made me uncomfortable. What I knew about teaching English told me that letting the breezes of imagination run through my own tales wasn't literature, and it wasn't teaching. Besides, it could lead to greater dangers. Students might take the wind into their own sails and journey solo across the storied seas. Out there they could meet all sorts of frightful possibilities—typhoon, doldrums, sea monsters, the edge of the earth! Understanding bloomed inside my head. As a student teacher I needed the freedom to fail in order to succeed. My students needed the same freedom, needed as I did to venture forth and confront demons. *For these are the stuff of myth,* the obstacles faced by heroes of all ages in search of their own meanings. The following day, I ran up the mainsail.

I decided to share with students the history of my own ambivalent relationship to ancient mythology. I told them how I had dreaded teaching *The Odyssey* at first (it was the one inflexible agenda item of my cooperating teacher's otherwise tolerant supervision). I told them how I had read a great deal, falling asleep over many a scholarly text, until I landed on Joseph Campbell's *Hero of Many Faces.* There I discovered connections between the myths of old and the stories I had heard growing up with a father inclined toward history, psychology, philosophy, and gab. Then I revised my own agenda, conceiving a project for my students that encouraged them to explore similar archetypes in their own family stories. Like the story quilt I had begun to piece together with a strand of Campbell's thread, their ideas about family lore, community legend, and imaginative hero parallels revealed the edge to a map of uncharted seas. Storytelling, like quilting and sailing, is an exploratory adventure, shot through with discoveries, improvisations, frustrations, and glorious epiphanies.

The new story in the wind would reveal itself only to the proper heir. My students embarked on a search for the extraordinary heroes of ordinary lives, for the legacies behind their own names and ethnic traditions. They interviewed parents and grandparents, wrote letters to distant relatives, dug into dusty photo albums and family papers. They researched cultural myths and the origins of names, traced the traditional hero's path through contemporary fiction and film, surveyed generations of American dreamers to map out the values of national, regional, and local communities. Some worked in groups, some in pairs, some set off alone. Some made videos—man-on-the-street interviews of what America means to you, a Hollywood collage of the American Dream. Some recorded oral histories; some illustrated family stories; others invented epics of their own. Throughout the project, we shared, compared, revised, and considered our findings in light of the old oral traditions. A groundswell of voices was building.

"My grandmother told my mother of this great man my mother never got to meet," wrote Tommy Harris, an affable student with a historical bent, "and in turn my mother told me. I will tell my kids, and teach the morals within the story. I deeply respect this hero and am proud to bear his name and tell his tale." From this beginning unfolded the epic, in improvised Homeric meter, of Edward (Thomas) Maxwell Holder, who in 1944 saved a drowning boy, only to die himself of a heart attack.

> The Youngest of eight,
> Hubert, Russell, Carroll the brothers
> Ella, Beulah, Bernice, and second youngest, Eva
> From them he soon earned the nickname Tommy
> From small Tom Thumb of children's story,
> . . . .
> On June 14th, at the lake of the camp
> A swimming boy of fifteen years
> got in trouble in the water
> And was close to drowning.
> Tom Holder knew he had to act
> Or the boy would die
> . . . .
> He dived into the lake
> And bravely towed the kid to land
> Others worked to revive the boy on shore
> In the midst of their frantic attempts at revival
> the rescuer was unnoticed missing
> . . . .
> Heroism had its rewards
> As well as its sometimes drastic price.
> Tom Holder lost his life that day
> But he also gained immortality.

Tommy's story was one of many that challenged the results of an earlier exercise in which many students had claimed that they had no heroes. It was also only one of many in which the hero turned out to be the author's kin. Several students wrote about ancestors' journeys to the New World or about the origins and meanings of their own names. Anna Maria Pellizzari, for example, wrote about her grandfather Pellizzari, "Fur Trader," who sailed from Italy with only the strength and convictions of his Catholic faith. He kept his epithetic name, but learned a new trade in the lumber industry. The Pellizzaris were fruitful and multiplied, carrying their name throughout the United States and eventually into the South. A third generation bore a daughter called Anna Maria, a name evoking the history of her forefathers and mothers—Grace, Rebel. Gracious Anna Maria rarely spoke in my class and answered most inquiries with a willing, demure smile. Rebel Anna Maria told us, "Sometime I'm noisy and boisterous. On the outside I may appear good and innocent, but I'm not always like that. . . . My last name connects me to my ancestors, it is something I share with them. It roots me to my heritage, making up my background, who I am, where I come from. Because I am so proud of it, I do not think I ever want to change it, even when I get married. It's not just my name, it's a part of me."

Continents away after World War II, Kavita Trivedi's parents grew up listening to the elders tell the age-old Hindu myth of Ganesh, the god with the elephant head. As adults, they migrated to America and bore a daughter who, steeped in the values and culture of the New South, neglected the old stories, the roots of her religious heritage. But like Anna Maria, Kavita rediscovered the ancestral gift and a new hero. Interviews with her parents, guided by well-thought-through questions, reincarnated Ganesh, the Master of Perfect Wisdom. The elders' teaching became part of our classroom: her father wrote to thank me for encouraging her to ask questions she had not asked before. Kavita retold the story of how Ganesh got his elephant head as a replacement for the one his father, Shankar, had cut off in a fit of jealous anger. "Hercules, too," Kavita noted in her paper, "got so mad and crazy that he killed his sons and wife. Both of these heroes were out of their minds when they committed their foolish acts." And their repentance afterward suggests that we must find ways to control our anger. Shankar's gift of the elephant head crowns his son with intelligence, discretion, balance, and patience. "I've learned what a perfect person should be like," Kavita concluded, "and now I have someone I can look up to, the Lord Ganesh."

The stories began to fly. My students dug deep into trunks and drawers; where they found only scraps, they improvised, quilting the tatters into new myths. Several students chose with my encouragement to write their own hero epics, taking into account the twelve steps of the hero we had discussed in class. Jesse Taylor, a shy introverted student, imagined the journey of a boy orphaned at the battle of Troy who seeks revenge against the evil Achaeans but finds instead wisdom and maturity. Andrea Goodrum, a prodigious writer given to political theses, created a heroine who gathers the child survivors of a nuclear holocaust and leads them to form a peaceful and cooperative society. Jay Joiner, an enigmatic smile in a tie-dyed shirt, invented a hero who is Underdog, Superman, and Magnum, P.I., all rolled into one. Jay gave his hero a mission that is a modern-day version of Hercules' tasks, but in this rewriting the tone is pure satire. Dirk Vice is "an average American middle-class clod." But like the mythological antihero Solo of George Lucas's *Star Wars,* Vice joins the cause of his fellow human beings. He becomes a crusader for endangered animals and for the environment—filling the hole in the ozone layer with car exhaust carried into the atmosphere by "Trojan double-ply, industrial strength, ribbed, lubricated, watermelon-flavored condoms."

Because I hoped that students would discover the archetypal journeys of myth and become conscious of how the literary choices authors make often reflect real-life concerns, I asked students who wrote fictional stories to attach to their work personal statements about how their stories reflected their own lives. Even teenage heroes must slay dragons in order to save the kingdom and save themselves. Jay's hero, the American Everyman, confronts the evils of industrialization. "I only hope there is a hero somewhere like Dirkman to set the wrongs in this world right," reflected his creator.

Michael Sanchez held up to his own adversaries the attributes of a hero he discovered in an ancient Mexican myth. "This story holds several morals for me," he commented. "One is that the biggest and strongest are not always the best. This is especially relevant to my participation in sports and helps me to remain optimistic when I see some of my opponents." Chris Schmid, author of a story about a hero named Norm, considered thoughtfully, "When I was trying to write this classic hero story, I decided to make my hero an average Joe. He wouldn't be some macho jock who rescued people regularly, he would be a man who was just like everyone else. I can relate this to my own life because I am just an average guy, and my dream is to someday do something that would make me heroic." When I pointed out that his hero's name was a particularly clever choice, Chris reeled. "I didn't even know I did that!" he stammered. "Maybe there is something to the meaning of names and all this subconscious stuff."

We had begun to discern the pattern of our quilt, to articulate the relationships among its many blocks. Square after square was recovered or remade from the fabrics of my students' four religions, three races, several cultures, the family quilts stitched by their mothers, preserved by their fathers. By sharing the projects in class through illustrated murals and group presentations and readings, at the same time that we studied *The Odyssey,* we wove them together with squares we found in the classic stories of Greek mythology. Perseus, Theseus, Penelope breathed deeply in the air of these modern legends. Temptation, loneliness, and monsters imagined and real threatened to break the life threads of heroes familial and mythical. In every environment, men and women searched for the narrow path between good and evil and yearned for honor. We journeyed both abroad and within, retracing the seeking steps of Telemachus. We followed Odysseus home for the great reunion. And we found in Ithaca a community of fourteen-year-old storytellers.

It's been two years since I finished my practicum, and the young voices of that classroom still mingle in my head with the rich Montana gloss of my father's stories. Teaching since, at both the high school and community college level, I have used storytelling more and more as the groundwork for units in narrative, oral history, autobiographical literature, mythology, and creative writing. I have discovered that students understand literature better when we allow it to be a launch pad into stories about students' own lives. I have concluded that students write more easily and are more willing to peer-workshop their writing when they have already told "the story" in small groups. I have found that students learn from my writing process, and by extension about their own, when I share with them my own true stories, seeds that germinate into poems, fiction, and essays. And most of all I have come to see the true value of storytelling—for myself as a teacher, for students, and for the classroom community—as a validation of the still, small voice within us all. When we tell a story, orally or on paper, we find something to say. When others listen, we delight in a feeling of importance and connection. When we listen to others, we learn to value our sameness and our differences. We gain a new appreciation, as participants, in the mythic heirloom of the ever-changing story quilt of human history.

Acknowledgments

This story is dedicated to the first storyteller in my life, my father, Hilton Vilen. I wish to thank many others whose voices are woven into the quilt: Dwight Rogers for encouraging the journal in which the story first unfolded; Henry Lister for insightful editing; Libby Vesiland for support and guidance throughout my student teaching and the revisions of this essay; and Hollace Selph for trusting me to tend the garden in which this story grew. I am especially indebted to Mrs. Selph's 1990–91 ninth-grade English classes, which provided the muse that continues to guide my learning about teaching.

15 Stories, Readers, and a Community of Learners

Julia Hamilton

Do you remember these opening lines?
" 'It was the best of the times, it was the worst of the times.'
" 'Call me Ishmael.'
" 'True! nervous—very, very dreadfully nervous I had been and am; but why WILL you say that I am mad?'
"Or even, 'It's been a quiet week in Lake Woebegon?' "

One of the things I teach my community college students to do in English 102, a course in which we read short stories and write essays about those stories, is to pay special attention to the beginnings of stories, to how a few words or lines can set a mood, develop an expectation, or establish a theme. Telling students about the power of first lines or pointing out how some beginnings work, like most lectures, has had limited effectiveness. So I ask students to prepare a brief story from their own experience to tell one another, usually in small groups and to take care to create an effective opening line. I have heard in their stories some pretty good first lines, such as "The sun sets early in winter here, so it was already dark when I walked to my car," or "I was surprised to find my dad at home that afternoon."

Later, when I ask students to reflect—in writing—on how they had gone about creating their opening lines and on what they had noticed about the opening lines of the stories they had listened to, most note how first lines work to get a story moving in a certain direction and are aware of why they had created the opening lines they did. They begin to read opening lines more slowly and with more attention to what those first few lines might be setting up for them as readers.

This initial telling of stories from their own experience with special attention to opening lines does more than give them insight into literary structure. The sharing of their stories in small groups introduces them to each other and starts the process of talking and listening to one another that will be essential if class discussions about literature and how we read and respond to literature are to develop and include everyone's perspective. Storytelling, then, in my classroom has become a way to teach certain concepts, a way to build a community of learners, and a way to teach a method of thinking.

When we begin talking about literary repertoires, what readers bring to the stories they read in terms of expectations of what literature "should be," I tell them a story as a way for them to become aware of how their prior experiences with literature are influencing the way they hear a story and how they respond to it. The story I tell is "Gawain and the Lady Ragnell," a version of "The Wife of Bath's Tale" set in King Arthur's Court. The tale has standard elements: a riddle (What do women desire most?) which must be solved under penalty of death; an unsuccessful, yearlong search for the answer; a loathsome hag who offers the correct answer in exchange for marriage with King Arthur's nephew; and a kiss which transforms a hag into a beautiful young woman at the end of the story.

After introducing the concept of literary repertoires but before I begin telling the story, I ask them to listen to this story in a special way: to note those places in the story where they thought they knew what was going to happen (for instance, they might be able to predict what color armor the evil knight would wear) and those places where they are surprised by a turn the story takes (they might not have expected the evil knight to ride away unharmed at the end).

Once I have finished telling the story, we begin our discussion by listing those elements which did and did not surprise us. The items in each list vary; most students will expect the hag to be turned into a beautiful woman, but some students will be totally surprised by Gawain's volunteering to sacrifice his freedom to save the life of his uncle, King Arthur. The latter students are usually unfamiliar with the courtly tradition of loyalty and honor. Then we begin to explore the differences in the lists: Why do the lists vary? What can the differences tell us about ourselves as readers? How do our expectations influence the way we respond to a story? How tolerant are we of stories that fit or do not fit our expectations? Even the beginning of the story, "Once, long ago in the days of King Arthur," sets off different responses in different students: some settle back, expecting a pleasurable experience, harkening back to childhood reading or storytelling, while others hear the "Once" as a signal that an irrelevant, most likely boring tale will follow.

When we begin these discussions, students typically respond in one of several ways. Some students just assume that whatever their expectations for the story are, everyone else's expectations will be the same. They assume that everyone has the same literary repertoire, and they may be uninterested in or dismissive of responses which differ from theirs. Others simply cannot see, or have difficulty seeing, that they even have expectations that influence how they hear or read a story; they assume the story just *is* and that they are only passively taking in the words. Other students seem convinced that a correct response or expectation exists, one which another student or the teacher has; they are willing to wait and listen for that sanctioned response. Gradually, however, after I show interest in the variety of expectations that students have and involve them in discovering where those expectations come from and how they might be influencing their responses to the story, they develop an interest in their own and each other's responses. They are on the path to becoming more reflective readers.

The discussion of how their expectations were or were not met as they listened to this traditional story allows students to understand how their literary repertoires affect how they understand and respond to what they read. They are not just taking in words; they are making meaning from what they read or hear based on their prior experiences. The goal is to make students more aware of how and why they respond in the ways they do; they begin to observe themselves in the very act of thinking.

Of course, I could pursue the same goal by having students read a story by themselves, but there is something, I think, in the communal act of telling a story to a group that helps students become aware that they are both listening to a story as individuals and as group members. I can interrupt the story, if I choose, to ask students what they think will happen next or what assumptions they have already made about a character, or I can ask which aspects of the story they are interested in—and by their various answers, students get an immediate sense of how their responses differ from or match the group's. They begin to see that some of those differences are related to age, sex, or culture. The immediacy of the oral setting allows all of us to experiment with new ways of examining how we are responding to a story. All of this, then, is a way of getting students to follow the dictum "Listen to how you listen," which is a precursor to getting them to become aware of how they read, of how they make meaning.

The next step is to follow the same process with a short story, and for my purposes and students', Joyce Carol Oates's "Where Are You Going, Where Have You Been?" works well. The strong plot line about Connie, a fifteen-year-old girl, and her encounter with Arnold Friend, who may be a fantasy, a seducer, or a murderer, provides both enough ambiguity and realism that students can explore their expectations for this story as they read. They follow the same procedure that they did with the story they listened to: as they read the story silently, they note how their expectations are or are not met as the story unfolds. To discuss their reading of the story and their expectations of it, we begin as we did with the Lady Ragnell story. What were their expectations? Where did those expectations come from? How did the expectations influence their understanding of the story? Then we entertain other questions. How might their expectations cause them to miss some things in the story or to interpret something in certain ways? What might be gained by examining their expectations and reading against those expectations? The goal is to provide more ways for students to see how reading a short story is an active venture in which they can participate more knowingly.

Student response to "Where Are You Going, Where Have You Been?" is usually varied and intense. Those students who decided from their reading of the text that Arnold Friend will rape and murder Connie are often astonished to hear that other students consider him a ridiculous but benign figure and that others think his visit to her house occurs only in Connie's imagination. Similarly, while some see Connie as a typical adolescent girl, others are critical of what they term her promiscuous behavior. Instead of encouraging the students to argue about the validity of their views, I ask students to construct a story, a chronicle, about how each of them read the text and how they came to view Connie or Arnold the way they did. What words or lines did they fasten on? What was happening in their minds as they turned the pages of the story? What were their assumptions as they read? They share their stories of how they read the text with one another in small groups. Everyone *has* a story about how he or she read the story, but initially everyone may not have an argument for a particular interpretation. Constructing a story of how they read the story and developed their interpretations seems to be an important step for many students to make before they can discuss the validity of their own or others' views. When students reread the text, they do so with an enriched view of what the story might be saying, and this occurs in large part, I believe, because they are encouraged first to explore their ideas in narrative rather than argumentative form.

On another day I assign students to read "Barn Burning" by William Faulkner, a story about a young boy, Sarty, who is caught between the tyrannical demands of his law-breaking father and his innate desire for justice and peace. The plot of the story is layered over with complex explorations of the social, historical, and psychological forces operating on the characters, and the omniscient narrator freely moves back and forth among the past, the present, and the future. The story, with its sophisticated vocabulary and convoluted plot, is a challenge for most college students to read. My assignment, though, is for them to come to the next class prepared to retell the story in their own words for the whole class. They protest; I insist.

At the next class I carefully choose four or five students to tell their versions of the story. On the basis of gender, sophistication, age, culture, or personality, I select students who I predict will have read and understood the story differently from one another. Assuring the storytellers that we will not be judging them on their storytelling ability and that they are part of an experiment on how we understand what we read, I usher these students from the classroom and then instruct the rest of the class to note what differences they hear in the stories as they listen to each version successively and to compare the versions they are hearing with the version they would have told. How did the teller begin the story? What did he or she emphasize? What was left out? How did the teller end the story?

Differences abound. One student focuses on the post-Civil War setting of the story and all its implications. Another student, a woman, comments on the sorry state of the female characters in the story. An older man tells the story with Abner, Sarty's father, as the main focus. A political science major emphasizes the class conflict between the poor whites and the aristocrats in the Old South. Another fastens on the poverty of the family and its effect on their intentions. The tellers even end their stories differently. Was there one gunshot or two? Is Abner dead or alive? What is Sarty's emotional state as the story ends? As the versions unfold before us, the evidence is clear; we have read different stories. Now, where did those differences come from? How can we begin to discuss a story which we have read so differently? As we explore those questions, we uncover several things. The way we read affects our understanding. Some students skip over unfamiliar words and historical references; others look them up. Others concentrate on dialogue and skip descriptive passages. Some details lodge in the mind; others do not. Some students are frustrated and even intimidated by challenging reading material; other students are more patient with themselves and the story.

Too, students see that when we read, we try to fit what we read into already established patterns. We look for the familiar. If we are used to discerning class distinctions, à la the political science student, we are more likely to see those distinctions than someone who is not so trained. We are reading stories with certain individually and socially constructed lenses that influence how we understand what we read.

As I walked down the hall last fall toward a class in which this retelling was to occur, one student, Tony, stopped me and begged me not to call on him that day—for the usual reasons; he wasn't prepared to tell the story. I agreed; he looked relieved. However, after the class in which we had listened to four versions of Faulkner's story and he had participated in discussing their differences and the implications for understanding how we read, I told him that I originally had planned to call on him and had wished he had been prepared. His reply, "I wish I had, too. I would have learned more," convinces me that telling stories, or in this case, retelling a story, works as a way for students to see that they read idiosyncratically. The energy that they put into shaping their stories for possible retelling and into noting the differences among the versions is almost tangible in the classroom. Again, I suggest that the immediacy of the telling-listening community heightens everyone's responsiveness.

So, how is it that students make use of this newfound knowledge about how they read and make meaning? The first step is to "listen to how they listen" or become aware of how they are reading and what they are bringing to the experience of reading a text. Storytelling can, in the ways I have described, help them do this. The next step is to share their responses, their readings, of literature with one another. If students can discern their own idiosyncratic readings and listen to others' readings with interest and appreciation, then they can use that enlarged viewpoint to go back to the story in question, reading it again from a wider, enriched perspective and looking for clarification and validation of their own and others' views.

One danger with a reader-response approach to literature is that the text will be entirely subordinated to the individual's personal agenda. (The danger in some other pedagogical and critical approaches is the opposite one: that the individual's response to a text will be subordinated to an official or scholarly view.) When students are first encouraged to air their individual responses, I find that they are quite happy to do so and, in their reading notes for example, write extensively about what memories a text generates, why they like a particular character, and what they are thinking and feeling as they read. But is this learning? For me as a teacher, the question becomes, am I teaching them anything that will stand them in good stead when they read another text in another classroom or outside the classroom? If they stop, or I allow them to stop, with just articulating their own responses, then I conclude that nothing much of value has occurred. Learning happens when students begin to listen to and seriously consider other, differing views, not as views that are automatically correct or sanctioned (like the teacher's) or wrong, but as evidence that individuals read, think, and approach problems differently. When this recognition happens, then I can say that a community of learners has developed in my classroom and that community has found a way to respond to and talk about literature and may have also found a way to think and talk about ideas and experiences outside the classroom.

The path that students usually follow is this one: first, they voice their response to literature and understand where that response is coming from; next, they learn to take others' views seriously; then, they are able to turn back to the text and read it with an enriched sense of what the text may be saying; finally, they are able to reach a conclusion about what the text may mean, grounding that understanding in the text and taking into account their own and others' responses to the text.

Storytelling, mine and theirs, in various ways throughout the quarter builds a sense of community; we listen together and we listen to each other. This practice in listening provides the basis for the conversations we can have about the stories we have read. Students, in effect, start out telling stories about how they have read the assigned texts and then move to discussing those readings. Students have to *have* a story to tell, an interpretation or reading of a text, before they can begin to discern differences in other readings and judge their validity. Storytelling, then, can be used in a literature classroom to help students develop their responses with others in ways that will enrich their understanding of a literary text.

I think of the way many students enter my classroom at the beginning of each quarter: shy, bored, anxious, estranged from each other and from the course material. They lack connections with one another, with me, and with the study of literature. And then I think of how I would like them to leave the room on the last day of class: at ease with one another and able to respond richly and reflectively to literature. I want students to tell their stories of who they are and how and what they think; I want them to find ways to connect their own worlds with the larger world that the study of literature and a college education represent. All too often they lack the means and experience to do so and settle back into silence. What I have found is that storytelling builds first a community and then a community of learners that can take into account each member's stories, and then asks them to account for or reflect on those stories. Storytelling provides the basis for our conversations with one another and about literature.

16 Let Them Tell Their Stories

Brian Conroy

In the middle of the suburban sprawl that is San Jose, California, there lies an oasis known as Katherine Smith Elementary. The riches and resources of this oasis are the students who have come to this special place from the far-flung corners of the globe. There are students here from China and India, from Nigeria and Nicaragua, from Malaysia and Indonesia. Students from Vietnam and Mexico, from Cambodia, Laos, Samoa, and the Philippines find a resting place at the oasis.

This tiny oasis in the midst of the suburbia which has grown around it is a few miles from the neighborhood where I was born. Growing up, I would have thought a place with such diversity very foreign indeed. But Katherine Smith Elementary, with its unique multicultural character, is unmistakably real.

Our staff members have always joked affectionately that we run a branch of the United Nations out of our school. In my fifth-grade classroom, with representatives from all over the world, it's not hard to imagine myself as Secretary General presiding over an international council.

Today I am blissfully conscious of the wealth I have been blessed with in having students from such varying cultural and linguistic backgrounds. My perception was not always so positive, however.

Not many years ago, I was getting so many conflicting messages about what the best strategies for teaching Limited English students were that I didn't know what to believe. I was inserviced in sheltered English, interactive writing, and multimodal instruction. My mind was boggled by the buzzwords of the day: "whole language," "invented spelling," and "integration." Then the State Department of Education sent a cordial message to my colleagues and me politely insisting that we integrate reading, writing, speaking, and listening in our teaching of language arts.

Right! With a predominance of students who have a fluency in the English language that includes a few survival phrases? Sure. No problem.

But then it hit me one day while I was serving yard duty at the ten o'clock recess that language is more than odd symbols on a printed page. Like a revelation from the ending of an Aesop fable, I was struck with the simple notion that a group of students having no similar vocabulary could communicate with each other perfectly well. There I was patrolling the perimeter of the playground, dreaming of summer vacation. Suddenly out of the corner of my eye I saw two students squaring off and landing the first blows in what each hoped would be an early knockout for the world title. In my role as peacekeeper and amateur referee, I hurried over to see if I could resolve the conflict diplomatically. I quickly separated the two boys, one of Mexican ancestry, the other of Vietnamese descent.

"Why were you fighting?" I asked.

Luis, the Mexican child, looked at me with matter-of-fact certainty and said, "He was swearing at me in Vietnamese!"

I shot a quick glance toward Huy, the Vietnamese child, who quickly bowed his head to the blacktop. Things looked suspicious, no doubt about it. I wasn't exactly sure what to say next.

Foolishly, I said, "Luis, you don't understand Vietnamese. How do you know what he said?"

Luis only cast his eyes downward. Suddenly both boys were silent, staring at their shoes, respectful of their teacher, but knowing the truth about a form of communication that went beyond words.

In that moment, some tiny door in my consciousness was opened. Here I was with two boys, both of whom spoke and understood very little English, yet each had been able to understand the expressions of the other in a foreign tongue.

Right then and there I realized that it wasn't so much what you said, but how you said it that mattered. My mind searched for alternative ways of expressing language. And the idea of storytelling stuck with me. Having enjoyed storytelling myself for many years, I found that it had the potential to transcend the confines of "vocabulary" and "comprehension." For storytelling, I found, was a way in which literature could be brought to life from a page in a text that might otherwise be frustrating or meaningless to Limited English students. The honesty of Luis and Huy had led me to believe that students telling their own stories was a classroom activity that could make language accessible for all students, if they were taught to tell stories with an emphasis on proper expression. For it was not Huy's words that Luis had understood, but rather his expressions and inflections.

For the rest of the year my students told story after story as part of language arts. We began telling stories as a group where all students joined in the telling, simultaneously using gestures, facial expressions, and movements to express the words and actions of the story. As we made these gestures, we would say the words of the story in unison. In making the gestures and movements, we gave the words of the story a concrete meaning that provided immediate understanding of the story.

We worked throughout the year with this type of "symbol language," standardizing a vocabulary of expressions which were given a practicality when applied to the words for which they stood. This simple activity sped up the process of language acquisition for the Limited English students and was a creative outlet for all students.

As the year progressed, we told tales by using manipulatives. With tales of this type, the focus of the story was shared between the storyteller and the particular type of manipulative which was used. We told tales with student-created felt characters which were put on a flannel board to illustrate the stories. We designed stories based on characters created out of tangram pieces and geoboard configurations. Interactive drawing and writing were used in creating and telling stories where one student would begin drawing or writing a story. The art work or writing of the story would be added to by other students until a short, simple story would be collectively created. We created stories through drawing cartoons, through drawing stories on scrolls, through creating dioramas. Stories materialized out of show-and-tell activities. We fashioned stories through forming cat's cradle figures out of string. We told stories by using magazine pictures and photos.

Next, as language fluency improved, we all learned to tell versions of a few common international folktales. Limited English students were taught the tales with the help of peer tutors, some of them who were able to translate in the students' native languages, others of them who used our preestablished "symbol language." Once students had an understanding of a tale, they had the choice of telling the tale to the class in either their own language or in English.

During that year we heard some of the more common folktales told in six or seven languages. And, as Luis and Huy had proven, virtually all of the children were able to understand the meaning of the tales, regardless of their language background.

Wonderful experimentation with language began to occur. Creative writing opportunities presented themselves spontaneously. We wrote modern versions of fairy tales, put ourselves into others, changed endings. We told stories from the point of view of another character with the story. After studying "how" and "why" tales or creation myths, we wrote our own myths and tales patterned after the ones we had learned. After learning to tell tall tales, we created our own tall-tale heroes, put them in modern circumstances in some cases, and told the tales to the class.

I had found an ideal way to integrate reading, writing, speaking, and listening with Limited English students, all as part of the same activity. When students were telling tales they were involved in speaking. Simultaneously the rest of the class was involved in listening. Whether translated, read, or told, the tales involved students directly with literature. Often they were provided with the text of the story they were to tell or were asked to write the text after their telling. Finally, there were writing activities before and after the tellings that ranged from summarizing and evaluating to the creative writing activities previously mentioned.

I found that students who had been silently floundering and felt themselves to be failures were speaking in English and in their native languages. They were actively engaged in literature in a way they perhaps never would have been had they not been given this opportunity. Language became more meaningful, understandable, fun. Consequently, students' appetites for reading increased as they discovered the source of reading and how rich it could be.

Things were going great. I was having an excellent year using storytelling. Just after the Christmas break, however, I received a new student. Duyen, from Vietnam, spoke a very limited amount of English and seemed somewhat intimidated by this whole storytelling business because she hadn't gotten off on the same foot as the rest of us. For weeks she was silent. Storytelling wasn't working for her. She spoke in class only a bare minimum, whether in English or in her native Vietnamese. A few weeks passed and quite by accident I asked one of my former students to teach me a song in Vietnamese. The only way I could learn the song was to write it out phonetically, using invented spelling. No doubt my pronunciation of the words was abominable. And so I went to the silent Duyen and asked her to help me with the pronunciation of the song. She immediately recognized the song and was eager to help teach me something from her culture. For a week or two we worked on that song together every recess and after school. Duyen meticulously corrected me on the most minute detail, forcing me to perfect my accent and translating the song for me during the process. For the remainder of the year Duyen opened up to the class and to me. She knew now that I respected her culture and that even teachers have weaknesses, especially when it comes to learning new languages.

Shortly after my "breakthrough" with Duyen, the class began a full-time campaign of collecting folklore. We collected directly from the community and found it brimming with folklore. We tapped the wellspring of folklore still alive and well in the memories of parents, relatives, and the students themselves. Not only were the tales we collected written in books handmade by the students, they were also told by the students who recorded them. With the help of student and parent translators, we collected seven books of folktales, superstitions, riddles, games, recipes, and songs, most of them recorded in English and the native language. At our school we no longer have a problem finding reading materials for students in their native languages. Over the past few years we have assembled a number of storybooks written in nearly every language represented at our school.

In addition to the telling of tales from oral and literary sources, we began to share personal stories throughout the year.

Once, as a storytelling assignment, I had students tell about their grandparents. A small, soft-spoken boy told about his grandmother who, as he said, was so tiny that, as he strolled around the block with her on their daily walk, everyone would make fun of his grandmother because she was so small.

"But I don't care," the boy confided, "as long as we can be together and be happy, that's all that matters."

Storytelling is one of the few activities that can evoke such feelings from students.

From personal stories to folktales to traditional stories that have yet to be recorded, the stories continue to be told on our little oasis in the middle of suburban San Jose.

And as I watch the San Jose of my youth transform into a growing and thriving showplace of cultural wealth, I have begun to understand the process of assimilation differently. For assimilation is a two-way street.

The story of America has always been the story of its immigrants. All of us, even Native Americans, were immigrants at one time. The immigrants' assimilation into American culture is simultaneously everyone's assimilation into world culture. In the give and take of cultural exchange, all of our stories are woven together into one great story quilt.

We, as teachers, must do our best to allow the new immigrants to tell their stories. If we share in this wealth of story and lore, all of our lives become enriched, ultimately creating a universal assimilation into the great multicultural family.

17 Teachers' Tales as Texts: Folklore and Our Profession

Bonnie S. Sunstein

The Pit. It is 6:45 a.m. In a windowless room, a dusty coffeemaker sputters its second pot. Six high school teachers have filled their mugs and settle around the stained formica table that is their morning support. This is the "Inner Pit," the physical and emotional core of the school building. Its very location is a metaphor. It is hidden in the inner hallway, inside another, larger room. Few students see the inner pit. Perhaps once it was a supply closet with shelves and a sink. Its bare cinder-block walls are painted yellow; two bulletin boards contain curled dittoed schedules, pink and green computer-made flyers advertise high school events, and slick brochures hawk opportunities for teachers in the outer world: European tours, study institutes at universities, government grants for independent study. There are ashtrays and an air filter, a phone, a few greeting cards and some cartoons on the wall. The "Outer Pit," a slightly larger room, holds a refrigerator, a microwave oven, two naugahyde sofas, a typewriter, a computer, and a ditto machine.

A group of people are in deep conversation. They are mostly middle-aged teachers, dressed in sweaters and skirts, or sport jackets and ties. On the table their black spiral plan books and red spiral rank books are bulging with piles of student papers. A man in his sixties, wearing a pin-striped suit, is bent over a set of papers, periodically writing red comments in student margins. He looks up occasionally. All the others are busy talking about the new English teacher:

"I heard Laurie had her coming-out party yesterday."

"Yes she did, her debut in the English department."

"I've been teaching seventeen years and it's going downhill now."

"Look at these gray hairs—each one has a kid's name on it."

"Like my weight," Donna quips, adjusting her sweater and tugging on her gold necklace.

The talk shifts to early teaching days, twenty years ago. Vivien talks about her first year of marriage, teaching in a small town. Her students would tell her they saw her wearing jeans; they asked if she was with her brother or her boyfriend, never guessing it was her husband: "In that little town, which by the way was a hop-growing center, teachers were told not to buy alcohol in any store in town or to drink in a local restaurant or bar. Seriously. I had to drive twenty miles to get a drink—which I needed because of my job." Sue describes going to the movies early in her teaching career. Her husband liked to sit near the front of the movie theater because of his bad eyes. He put his arm around her chair, and they heard a loud, collective "WHOA" from behind, trailed by muffled giggles.

Ruth tells about going to the thirtieth high school reunion of her first English class in the town where she began teaching. "I was their class adviser. Except for the one who died, they are no different now than they were then. One guy was practically kneeling at my feet because I passed him. There was Charlie Pico, with the black shirt, the neck chain, the permanent—at forty-seven years old."

Vivien offers a story, from an ex-colleague in another school: "At the end of the year when we were pretty sick of kids and vice versa, and they were off the wall, Roy Rose used to say, ''You know, if we'd just shoot one of 'em in September and let him hang in the cafeteria awhile, we wouldn't have any trouble all year."

In a few seconds on a random morning, these teachers have defined themselves as "experienced and old," setting themselves apart from the new teacher who has just had her "coming out," her initiation into the school. They associate gray hairs, weight gain, the initiation story about Laurie, and their years of teaching with their occupational expertise. They cannot touch their husbands, they cannot drink; they learn early in their careers that teachers are expected to maintain a pure public persona. Ruth's Charlie Pico story reminds everyone that teachers' control of students lasts far beyond their high school years. At his thirtieth reunion, decked out in slick garb, Charlie was still a supplicant, and Ruth was still in control. Vivien's image of a hanging student is outrageous; it is an absurd reminder of the unpredictable. Already, the stories have defined personal initiations into the profession and the serious responsibilities they take for the lives of students.

As the conversation continues, they tell stories about failed students. One is about a student named Matthew, who graduated a few years ago. One of the teachers saw him working at a local gas station. "Sally Stephens says he's one of the most well-read students she's ever had . . . I had him one year, and I failed him the second year. I had to keep failing him because he kept failing himself." They discuss Matt's marriage to Tracy and their baby. "She can't hack it with the baby," another teacher says. Sally comments: "It was so funny because he was so against authority in general, but not against an authority figure. He was never angry at me, just angry at the system." She reports that she had taken her car in and Matt had balanced her tires—just after he had called her "bitch" in class. She concludes, "But I like Matt, and I'm sorry."

The teachers in the Pit agree, Matt had an unhappy beginning. And another story genre is born: the "good student gone wrong." Two girls became hairdressers: "By May of their senior year, neither one had gotten into the college she wanted, and I think they just never recovered. Tricia was one of my best writers," Ruth says, "I thought God, honey, you just cut off your options for your whole life, and here you are not more than twenty-one."

With the tenderness of parents, the compassion of counselors, the sharp-witted detailing of scholars, the earthy humor of TV comedians, these teachers perform their "shared progeny" stories, developing more genres as they swap observations. The students' problems exist outside the culture of the school; the teachers have done the best they can, and after the students leave them, teachers can only observe and document their fate.

A large man walks in. "Did you know that Ruth and I are having an affair? That was before she stopped drinking and switched to pills." He sits down on one side of Ruth. She sits at one side of the table, her soft salt-and-pepper hair morning-neat; her teal eye shadow is a striking complement to her purple turtleneck. She sits straight; her hands are folded over her completed paper work tucked neatly in carefully labeled folders.

On the other side of the table, the silent social studies teacher puts away his papers, opens his mythology book, and shows a picture of women wrestling with two bulls. "That does something to me," he says. "Here's a cartoon of a woman taking a bull by the horns, and Ruth thought it was a man." Ruth takes a lot of ribbing. She is fifty-two years old, a minister's wife, and she admits she's been a "goodie-goodie" all her life. The others know it, but they also know she can tease right back. She tells a story about when Bob complained he had taught a history lesson badly: "Bob likes to make big pronouncements that shock people and he likes to brag about never doing any work. It was interesting to me that somebody pointed out that his students know an awful lot about American history. And so after having lunch with him several days in a row in which he bragged that he didn't do this and he didn't do that, I finally said to him, 'Bob, you're just full of shit, that's all.' He was in a state of shock."

"Is this Sex 101?" Lorraine, the librarian, enters the Pit. She washes her hands and pours herself some coffee. It is 7:05 now, twenty minutes after the first coffee was poured. Ruth is the first to leave. She scoops up her books, washes her cup, carefully places it upside down on a paper towel, and walks briskly to her room.

With their stories, Ruth and her colleagues in the Pit define their occupational culture, share their anxieties, confirm their positions, evaluate each other's and their students' performances in a complex and quickly moving routine. In a short twenty minutes the vigorous exchange of narratives helps them collect themselves before they face hall duties and homerooms, scholarship and spitballs; seven hours of maintaining a public persona in the faces of energetic adolescent students, inside their carefully prescribed institutional responsibilities.

The Project

Why does this look so familiar? Where have we heard these stories before? What strategies do we use to handle the thousands of human stories that pass in and out of our lives and our schools from year to year? What is the social glue that holds our profession together? What's the value of the stories we share with each other? What can we learn about ourselves as teachers, our relationships with students, our lives inside our institutions by sneaking glimpses of our own storytelling traditions?

This conversation in the Pit holds some clues. Teaching is a complex human profession that must be grounded on the sturdiest of scholarship and the most knowledgeable blending of theory and practice. But peeking through the smoke into the teachers' room and listening after the bell rings at 2:56 p.m., we realize there is another dimension to study. Here, we can see teachers in the act of what sociologists Berger and Luckman (1977) call the social construction of reality. When we see our lives as a social community, we enter what Bruner calls "a folk culture" (1990, 14), rich in storytelling genres, deep in the traditions of our elders, defined by crafts that are special to our profession. We guide our initiates with sympathetic humor, jab at our peers with sarcasm, and nod to our mentors with respect. The very nature of teachers and our utterances—the "performance"—helps to shape our shared self-awareness.

I was curious to look carefully at this oral culture of ours, and to do it, I used the discipline of folklore studies, which learns from people's spoken texts. When a group tells stories in an occupational setting, folklorists call it verbal art (Bauman 1975). Like the audiences listening to the tales told in ancient oral cultures, our teacher-audiences are informed: they share the language, rituals, pranks, and habits of our occupational culture. Each telling is a performance; the audience can respond, react, and reevaluate. "In some sense," folklorist Oring suggests, "for something to be folklore in an urban society, it must be touched and transformed by common experience—ordinary humans living their everyday lives" (1986, 16). Folklorists document a performance in a work culture by looking for "cultural scenes," the recurrent social situations, the daily rituals in which workers share their cultural knowledge or their folklore. I found one such place in the Pit, and I created another at an informal get-together at my home.

Both the teachers' room and the informal party are tension relievers; the stiff public persona demanded of teachers can relax, their behavior can soften. In the case of the Pit, the shared culture is that of the institution. The context level in a teachers' lounge is high; their stories are about relationships among a familiar set of characters; they define the history of that high school and its students. Their stories and language confirm each other's concerns and identify the boundaries of acceptable behavior within the institution itself.

But at the party at my house one night, the terms, stories, and jokes defined the professional boundaries of the teaching of English. Although these teachers had never worked together, within minutes their shared occupational culture opened a treasury of stories, embellished with common attitudes and experiences.

The Pizza Party

To see another context of occupational storytelling, I gave a party, an "induced natural context," in the language of folklorists (Goldstein 1964, 25). I invited five English teachers, including Ruth, to my house. I selected them because they were all experienced and articulate; they did not know one another. They ranged in age from thirty-two to fifty-two; they had taught in Nova Scotia, Massachusetts, New Hampshire, New Jersey, Ohio, Iowa, Oregon, and Washington. Some were single, some were married, some had children, some did not. These six people had only one common feature: they all had been high school English teachers for more than five years. I paid for the pizzas and placed my tape recorder in the middle of the dining room table. It didn't take long before we were swapping stories. The jargon flew around the table before I had finished pouring the wine.

Like the teachers in the Pit, we described our early days in teaching, the sicknesses and tensions. Valerie had lost so much weight she went on a high-protein food diet. She managed to make it through her first year, but her mother had to cook high-protein food, and she took five meals a day to school. Ruth's husband pushed her out of the car every morning, and she was treated for anemia. Nancy began teaching in her home town; her little sister was in her first class. Everybody cried—all the time.

We all began our teaching with an inordinate number of "low groups" and all the challenges associated with them, the oldest grammar books in the book closet, unheeded threats of low grades, assignments undone, classes unattended, drugs detected, detentions unserved, switchblades in boots. We joked about advice from wise old practitioners, and the proverbs emerged in our talk:

> *Jane:* People said, "Don't judge teaching by your first year," so I believed them.
>
> *Meg:* Never flunk anyone you can't stand, because they'll be back.
>
> *Nancy:* Never have a child in your class who's smarter than you are. If you have someone in your class who's smarter than you are, transfer them out. Well, I had a lot to transfer out.
>
> *Bonnie:* And how did you measure whether a kid was smarter than you?
>
> *Nancy:* Oh, I could tell right away. For one, they weren't teaching, and had no intentions of ever doing so.

The stories began to flow as the wine bottle emptied. The stories appeared in genres: they defined practices, passions, philosophies, fears, and living nightmares. They supported our common love of words: books, writing, reading, poetry, even grammar. They supported our common love of students: "After my first year, I knew I'd never go back to something routine. For every seventeen I'd have murdered, there were seventeen that kept me going," Valerie said. These are the students who come back to visit years later, whose literacy accomplishments we want to take partial credit for: the published writers, the English professors, the actors, the scholars. There were stories of bad administrators, stories of raucous pranks, but most of the stories clustered into the following eight categories.

Doing Something Terrible to a Set of Papers Stories

Meg had a car accident; she rolled her car over into a cow pasture, and the first thing she did after emerging from the car was to collect a set of final exams yet to be graded. A man came over to see if she was okay, and she screamed "Grab those papers!" They were crusty with cow manure, but she handed back every one. Nancy had done a beautiful sound-slide presentation with a class, a project that had taken months and a lot of money. She put it in the trunk of her car over the weekend, went to a conference, and the project disappeared. Jane's "low-level freshmen" had written beautiful, illustrated children's books and were about to take them to the local elementary school to read one-on-one with children. She had set them, tenderly and organized, in a carton next to her desk, and discovered the next day that the custodian had thrown them out. I completed a set of report cards while I was in labor with my first child—counting contractions and students at the same time, in fear of my vice principal's wrath. Ruth had passed out a set of papers to another teacher's class without recording the grades. But the most graphic story, the one which represents every teacher's fear, was this one of Valerie's: "I had this stack of papers that I had been putting off for the longest time, and I had promised that they'd be back the next day. I was sitting there, drinking a glass of wine. It was Christmastime, and I had a candle on the table, and damned if I didn't set the whole bunch on fire."

Through our recounting of the nightmares of losing student papers, we defined the importance of our students' work and our own vulnerability as people in control of these "stacks" of human productions. These stories emerged as a genre, as well as an important way for us to share our collective respect for our own and our students' productions.

What to Do When a Student Won't Do Homework Stories

At the opposite pole from our responsibility for students' work, when students don't do homework, teachers need to let them know the consequences. In this discussion, we shared stories of our schools' homework policies, the problem of parents away from home, our administrations' backup systems, the students who keep forty-hour-per-week jobs and are pressured with sports and the other academic disciplines. Reading and writing time is too hard to measure and predict, we agreed, so students often ignore it. We considered the ethics of passing students just so that we would not see them again. Do we let them out in society? Do we keep them in until they drop out? A whole class cheered when one of Jane's students turned in his first paper in the spring. Valerie flunked a senior who was signed up with the marines. His parents tried to bribe her, then threatened to take her to court; she retracted her *F.*

But most of the stories were about undone homework: "I remember this real cute little fellow I had who was a real good student, and he said, 'Miss Williams, I think we should settle something right away, okay, I do lots of writing, I like to write, but I don't write essays.' And I said, 'But we have some essays, Robbie.' And he said, 'Well, I don't write essays.' And I said, 'Well, I don't pass kids who don't write essays. As long as we understand each other, Robert. . . .' "

Enjoying the Joy of Colleagues Stories

"All my teaching friends loved books, and we always shared them, so you were always right on top of new reading." Each of us belonged to writing groups, as teachers or students, in school and out, and we shared the experience of having attended summer writing programs in the early 1980s, when we were able to do our own writing in the company of other teacher-writers. Although the writing groups were all in different places, the six of us were all in summer programs within a few years of each other, a time that marked a change in most people's approaches to teaching writing. We told stories of "conversion experiences," transformations of ourselves as writers.

How to Work with Current Techniques
in the Real Classroom Stories

We talked about fitting the study of grammar into current approaches to writing; what we still do that would offend the "process purist." "It seemed that the kids who were the poorest writers knew the most grammar," Nancy said. When we had to teach grammar, we would take a few days just to do it. Jane would use ditto sheets with examples from kids' writing; Ruth discussed her frustration that there were no "exact steps" to follow and that it was supposed to be healthy to find them herself. "That's where the process falls down in the classroom," she noted. "A misinterpretation that can grow out of the one-hour workshop," added Meg. "And a lot of it comes from the early literature that never dealt with 'how do you teach kids that there are sentence fragments and they probably ought to try to avoid them, and stuff like comma splices.' " Ruth said, "Without instruction, there is no language, there are no labels." Nancy commented, "Yes, it gives you a language to talk about the language with."

We went on to discuss sentence combining as a technique for letting the language evolve, and the current ideas about teaching literature; that students need to "discover" meaning in a text. "I very quickly realized that they weren't going to talk about literature the way that we had talked about it in university English classes," Nancy said. "You might as well just throw that out. And there was no point in my telling them how to think about it, I knew that wasn't the point, I was trying to get them to write about these things critically. So I did a little experiment with a bunch of grade 10 students: We'll see what they can do if *they* talk about the book, and I don't ask questions or draw their attention to things, or whatever. And it was amazing because they knew all the right things to do. So that was kind of my beginning of reader-response."

Teaching Common Literature Stories

Our discussion slid easily into teaching literature with a story about Tim, a friend of Jane's who had pulled a prank on one of his friends by taking over his class one day when the students were reading "Bartleby the Scrivener." Tim constructed an entire lesson based on the symbolism of the letter *B* in the story, and when his friend later tested the students, they all wrote essays about the *B* symbols in Melville.

Ruth described her colleague next door, who works with *Beowulf:* "Mike wanted to find a way to bring the kids to the text, and he talks to them about being an encoder and a decoder . . . he has neat little funny exercises about talking to parents and teachers, and then when he gets to *Beowulf*, he draws pictures, and he puts all the parts of the culture in, like the mead hall, and the warriors, and he makes this little tiny woman. She's tiny because she's the only woman, and only mentioned once—the queen that pours the mead."

Meg: Freeawaru?

Bonnie: Freeawaru!

Jane: My God, they remember her name.

Nancy: I translated it, and I don't remember.

"Isn't it true that you don't really know something until you teach it?" I asked. Nancy answered, "Boy, I'm sure I could do *Romeo and Juliet* right now." Jane remembered, "That used to be my favorite thing, when I'd walk into the classroom, and they'd be rowdy, I'd say, 'Rebellious subjects, enemies to peace.' " We all joined in, laughing, and finishing the lines from *Romeo and Juliet*: "Throw your mistemper'd weapons to the ground. . . . And hear the sentence of your moved prince. . . ."

> *Meg:* My favorite was "She speaks yet she says nothing."
> *Nancy:* They didn't get that.

We told literature stories until it became very serious inquiry: "Is it personality that makes a teacher present material a certain way?"

"Is it a 'sifting' of everything they've been exposed to before?"

"Isn't it that you're not teaching literature, you're teaching people?"

"Dewey, I'd say, would say you're teaching both: the whole point is literature meeting the people."

"I think part of it's personality, but I think it's also partly the way that we feel about literature, and we know that books aren't in vacuums. They are about real people in real situations in certain time periods, wearing certain clothing, and in a certain culture, and rather than being dead on a page, you might want to do some of these other things that make the kids as excited about it as you are, and *how* you do it has to do with your personality. But there's nothing worse than having a book you love be just another book."

"I always felt a real kinship with some authors, that I was the only channel for these particular kids to make this guy's life worth something. I'm somehow introducing him to them."

Valerie says, "I always think fondly of Ezra Pound's last words that what hell it was to start with a swollen head and end with swollen ankles. How poignant that was—that you always try."

Reading Things That Make Us Cry Stories

Telling stories about crying in front of classes brought tears of laughter, at ourselves and our stories. Valerie cried each time she read the poem "The Harpweaver." I cried reading "The Man Without a Country" to eighth graders, although I complained about teaching it in the sixties when nobody wanted to admit to patriotic feelings. Nancy cried yearly over Truman Capote's "A Christmas Memory"; Ruth over "Bill" by Zona Gale. Of course, each teacher was moved by a different piece of literature, but the most hilarious performances for us were in our stories about students' reactions to our tears:

" 'What did she have in her eye?' "

"Some of them laugh."

"Some of them cry."

"Some look down."

"Some say, 'What's wrong with you? It can't be something you're reading.' "

In these little admissions, we reconstructed our reality and shared our vulnerabilities. Like the traditional informed audiences of ballad singers, our students helped to shape our performances.

Avoiding Unintended Sexual Undertones Stories

Another pattern that emerged in the stories was teachers' changing words while reading aloud to avoid giggling with the students. Our public persona was far too stiff to stand adolescent giggles. We admitted many stories about changing words and phrases. It always began, we agreed, with unintended sexual undertones. I remembered my department chair who said, "Just don't ever bother teaching lie and lay; it's not worth the class period of giggling."

> *Meg:* Once when I was subbing, I said, "I don't know anyone's name so I'm going to have to take roll orally."

> *Jane:* In *Our Town,* on the wedding morning, George Gibbs has got to run over to see Emily, and his mother says "Don't forget your rubbers." I *always* just changed it to "galoshes."

> *Valerie:* In *Alice in Wonderland,* she has a piece of cake that says "Eat Me." I don't bother with that part.

> *Bonnie:* I always substitute "chest" for "breast" in poetry, no matter what it does to the syntax or the alliteration or the assonance. I just have to.

> *Nancy:* Every grade 10 student I've ever taught *Macbeth* to remembers "Come ye ministering spirits, unsex me, change my mother's milk. . . ." They like Shakespeare.

> *Meg:* As soon as they know what "biting their thumb" at each other means, they're okay.

> *Ruth:* Yes, you see them going down the hall: "You bit your thumb at me, sir?"

Meg: The first time I was ever observed, we were reading "The Wife of Bath's Tale." And, of course, I got to that line, and I was reading aloud: "And lo, he took her maidenhead," and someone said immediately, "What's that mean?" And the vice principal, who had been dozing in the back of the room, snapped to attention. Another kid said "It means he cut her head off." I said "He did something to her, but it wasn't that." The kid said "He raped her!" It was the first question they'd asked in twenty-five minutes, and the vice principal said it was the only interesting English class he'd ever observed.

One-Upping the Kids Stories

Valerie talked about a student who wore a headset every day, sat on the back of a chair until she told him to get down, and wore a camouflage outfit, so she would mark him absent. Ruth said that she always tells her students that if she's the biggest problem they'll ever have, they'll be lucky in life. Meg ended her exams with "These are the best days of your life." Ruth told about a student who said, "This library doesn't have crap," to which she answered, "Libraries don't usually stock that." Nancy remembered a student whom she would have liked to throttle. "It didn't seem to matter. I tried talking to him, I tried doing all these different things, and none of it worked. We just didn't hit it off. He just decided on day one. Anyway, I was handing back something or other that they'd written, I guess, and he hadn't handed it in. I said, 'John, I have to give you a zero for that because you didn't do the work and you're not going to get through English by not doing the work,' and he just looked at me and he said, 'That's all right. I'm going to be a stud when I grow up,' and without missing a beat, I said, 'Well, you'll starve, then.' "

To Sum It Up

Admitting the importance of sarcasm, irony, and our need to create it was one more way we "constructed our reality" that evening. Our verbal art was clear, that we shared it was even clearer—six teachers who had forged six very different careers over long periods of time, in distant places. We used the same language, shared the same core of common values and materials, enjoyed both listening and performing as we shaped each other's occupational lore. That night, we represented the community of English teachers to one another and ourselves.

Meg remembered, "When I was majoring in drama, whenever we walked off stage, we'd go into the green room. You drop your character, have a smoke, and wait for your next cue. It's very much like it is in teaching. You're on stage all day, playing a role to an extent. You have to be so correct, have the right reactions, look shocked and get mad if someone swears. When the bell rings, you can go into the teachers' room and be yourself. Have a smoke, say 'shit' if you want to. I think that's why faculty rooms are so crazy. It's a chance to be offstage."

As each other's audiences, our reactions are part of the act of our creations; our shared knowledge sets the genres of our stories, our dialogue touches the borders. Here, in folklorist Dundes's words, "The telling is the tale; therefore the narrator, his audience, and his story are all related to each other as components of a single continuum, which is the communicative event" (1964, 263). In our storytelling, there is "no dichotomy between process and product," our process is our product; we reshape our occupational borders as we tell our stories.

The pizza party and the Pit are both places where the process of being a teacher takes place. We need each other's stories in order to define our performances, understand our audiences, and, most important, to inquire about and better understand what it is that we do. In the private company of others who must maintain the same public persona, we can ground our reality and blend our theory and practice. After the last bell rings, between classes, inside our private spaces, our shared occupational knowledge is a precious and dynamic tool for relieving tension, defining context, forming inquiry, and improving our work by transforming our understanding of our culture in the stories we tell.

Resources for Storytellers

The Art of Storytelling

Baker, Augusta, and Ellin Greene. 1987. *Storytelling: Art and Technique.* 2d ed. New York: Bowker.

A comprehensive overview of the world of storytelling in libraries and schools, with specific techniques for learning how to become a storyteller. Augusta Baker is a major early figure in storytelling in America.

Barton, Bob. 1986. *Tell Me Another: Storytelling and Reading Aloud at Home, at School, and in the Community.* Portsmouth, N.H.: Heinemann Educational Books.

Tips and techniques for storytelling and reading aloud. The book includes many full-text stories with games and poetry that make excellent "stretchers" between stories. Follow the suggestions in Chapter 3, "Making the Story Your Own," and you'll never worry about forgetting your story as you tell it!

Bauer, Caroline Feller. 1977. *Handbook for Storytellers.* Chicago: American Library Association.

This enjoyable and practical book is a must for storytellers or would-be storytellers. Part Four of the book contains a section entitled "Programs," which gives examples of how storytelling can be integrated into the school curriculum. Bauer is known for her effective use of realia, or props, in storytelling; she shares many creative ideas for using realia in Part Three, "Multimedia Storytelling." Brimming with enthusiasm, the book is filled with practical, interesting, tried-and-true activities and suggestions.

Breneman, Lucille N., and Bren Breneman. 1983. *Once Upon a Time: A Storytelling Handbook.* Chicago: Nelson-Hall.

With chapter headings like "Choosing a Story," "Working for Characterization," and "Anticipating a Real Audience," these master storytellers and teachers take readers through a comprehensive tour of the world of storytelling performance. They use simple language, concrete examples, and positive words of encouragement to train would-be tellers. Read the whole book and then zero in on problem areas like stage fright, volume control, and memorization. The book works well as a classroom tool or do-it-yourself handbook.

Bruchac, Joseph. 1987. Storytelling and the Sacred: On the Uses of Native American Stories. *The National Storytelling Journal* (Spring):14–18.

An important article for anyone who is contemplating telling a Native American tale. The article reviews some of the concerns which arise for many Native Americans when non-natives tell tribal stories. Issues concerning the traditional use of stories interweave with issues relative to Native American religious practices. Bruchac offers excellent suggestions about how to learn and tell tribal stories and about the types of stories to avoid.

Cooper, Pamela J., and Rives Collins. 1992. *Look What Happened to Frog: Storytelling in Education.* Scottsdale, Ariz.: Gorsuch Scarisbrick Publishers.

An up-to-date, concise overview of how and why to tell stories in educational settings. There are also more than seventy-five pages of storytelling activities for all ages and levels of tellers, tips on finding your own voice, profiles of storytellers, and a reference and resource section. An excellent choice for an introductory text.

Horne, Catherine. 1980. *Word Weaving: A Storytelling Workbook.* San Francisco: Zellerbach Family Fund.

An excellent resource of suggestions and activities for developing storytelling skills, including introductory activities and ideas to prime an audience for listening to stories. Many full-text stories are included.

Livo, Norma J., and Sandra A. Rietz. 1986. *Storytelling: Process and Practice.* Littleton, Colo.: Libraries Unlimited.

From the functions of storytelling to tips and techniques for storytelling, this book is a classic for anyone wishing to develop art and technique. Livo and Rietz write from a lifetime of storytelling experience to give a very practical and comprehensive guide. Those interested in developing storytelling workshops for students or adults will also find this book helpful.

Maguire, Jack. 1985. *Creative Storytelling: Choosing, Inventing and Sharing Tales for Children.* Cambridge, Mass.: Yellow Moon Press.

Maguire covers everything from the purpose and values of telling stories to traditions, tellers past and present, finding stories for different aged children, enhancements such as games or poetry, and the creation of one's own stories. An excellent resource for the beginning storyteller, giving enough information to get you started but not too much to overwhelm you. A real help to the teacher-storyteller.

Neale, Robert E. 1991. *Tricks of the Imagination.* Seattle, Wash.: Hermetic Press.

The subject of this book is performing magic with stories, and

Neale says that it is also a celebration of the telling of tall tales. The author presents twenty-five stories that are wound around pieces of magic. The accompanying magic is explained in detail, and most of the tricks involve everyday objects such as playing cards, pebbles, rope, coins, and newspapers, although sometimes pieces of specially designed apparatus are used (one of which is included with the book). Experienced magicians will find many of the tricks familiar, but each one has been reworked by Neale for maximum effect and to help tell a compelling tale. The tales themselves are the focus here; Neale suggests that all of them be read before reading any of the explanations of accompanying magic tricks, because the stories themselves are the real magic.

Pellowski, Anne. 1987. *The Family Storytelling Handbook: How to Use Stories, Anecdotes, Rhymes, Handkerchiefs, Paper and Other Objects to Enrich Your Family Traditions.* New York: Macmillan.

Simple and easy-to-follow advice on why, when, what, and how to tell stories in family settings. An anthology of stories for the very young is included, along with stories told with handkerchiefs, origami, paper cut or torn, fingers, and objects, and stories drawn in sand, snow, or mud.

Ross, Ramon Royal. 1980. *Storyteller.* 2d ed. Columbus, Ohio: Merrill.

Although the book is out of print, it is available in many libraries. An excellent resource for how to tell stories, including specific steps for developing stories for the flannel board.

Sawyer, Ruth. 1942/1969. *The Way of the Storyteller.* New York: Viking Press.

A classic. Written when Sawyer was sixty-two, this book contains the wisdom of a lifetime of storytelling. Written with sensitivity to the tale and audience. Sawyer includes the texts of some of her own favorite stories.

Schimmel, Nancy. 1982. *Just Enough to Make a Story: A Sourcebook for Storytelling.* 2d ed. Berkeley, Calif.: Sisters Choice Press.

This sourcebook, written by an experienced professional storyteller, contains suggestions for choosing, learning, and telling stories. It's an excellent introduction for beginners and a source of new ideas for those in need of refreshment. There's an assortment of stories suitable for different grade levels, as well as lists of appropriate stories for adults. With the authority of someone who knows what children love to hear, Schimmel discusses picture books, songbooks, records, and finger puppets. An extensive list of sources of nonsexist stories with active female protagonists is included. *Just Enough to Make a Story* is the kind of resource one refers to over and over to freshen technique or update material.

Schwartz, Marni. 1990. The Silences between the Leaves. In *Workshop 2,* edited by Nancie Atwell. Portsmouth, N.H.: Heinemann Educational Books.

> In this article the author traces her history with one tale, learning about it and from it, thus providing insight into deepening one's experience with a particular story. The title comes from a poem about knowing something well.

Shedlock, Marie L. 1952. *The Art of the Story Teller.* 3d ed. New York: Dover Publications.

> A reprint of a work originally published in 1915. Based on Shedlock's lectures to teachers in America and England, this book provides a master class in storytelling, followed by an anthology of stories.

Sierra, Judy, and Robert Kaminski. 1991. *Multicultural Folktales: Stories to Tell Young Children.* Phoenix, Ariz.: Oryx Press.

> Twenty-five folktales from around the world appropriate for telling to young children. The book is divided into four parts: Storytelling Techniques and Materials, Folktales for Ages Two and a Half to Five, Folktales for Ages Five to Seven, and Resources for Storytelling. The text of each story is followed by sections that include tips for learning the story and how to tell the story with flannel board or puppets. Many patterns for simple puppets are included. Three of the Hispanic stories appear in Spanish.

Storytelling in the Classroom

Barton, Bob, and David Booth. 1990. *Stories in the Classroom: Storytelling, Reading Aloud and Role-playing with Children.* Portsmouth, N.H.: Heinemann Educational Books.

> This work, specific to classroom settings, continues Barton's earlier work listed under "The Art of Storytelling."

Cather, Katherine D. 1922. *Education by Story-Telling: Showing the Value of Story-Telling as an Educational Tool for the Uses of All Workers with Children,* edited by C. W. Hetherington. Yonkers-on-Hudson, N.Y.: World Book Co.

> A part of the Play School Series, based on the work of the Demonstration Play School of the University of California. This comprehensive text covers the how-to aspects of storytelling, along with extensive discussion of its benefits and uses across the curriculum. Early chapters focus on developmental story interests of young children. An anthology of stories is included, along with lists of stories to tell by months of the school year.

Cooper, Pamela J., and Rives Collins. 1992. *Look What Happened to Frog: Storytelling in Education.* Scottsdale, Ariz.: Gorsuch Scarisbrick Publishers.

> See annotation in "The Art of Storytelling" section.

DeWit, Dorothy. 1978. *Children's Faces Looking Up: Program Building for the Storyteller.* Chicago: American Library Association.

> What a book! Excellent ideas for building storytelling programs with ready-to-use examples. Section Six provides suggestions for how to shorten stories that are too long.

Hamilton, Martha, and Mitch Weiss. 1990. *Children Tell Stories: A Teaching Guide.* Katonah, N.Y.: Richard C. Owen Publishers.

> These authors are known as Beauty and the Beast Storytellers. They have drawn on their experience as freelance tellers to develop this excellent guide for teachers who want to help children tell their own stories. A major portion of the book is devoted to a unit of instruction on storytelling for elementary school children. It contains twenty-five stories appropriate for beginning tellers, along with activities to develop storytelling skills. Guides for storytelling units are also included.

Lipman, Doug. 1986. Story Games: Part I. *The National Storytelling Journal* 3(4):24–26.

> Lipman describes the procedures for and the values and possible adaptations of six story games. The games are based on popular parlor games of long ago, but are easily incorporated into a process-writing approach. The games provide students with opportunities to generate stories orally in a game format just as they would in the prewriting phase of process writing. Part II of this article appears in volume 4, number 1, pages 12–17 of the same journal.

Livo, Norma J., and Sandra A. Rietz. 1987. *Storytelling Activities.* Littleton, Colo.: Libraries Unlimited.

> A highly practical collection of activities that connect to various aspects of storytelling. Material included focuses on finding and creating stories to tell, coming to understand story patterns and structures, and techniques for story presentation and delivery. Activities offered are appropriate for all ages and can be used in a wide variety of settings.

Mallan, Kerry. 1991. *Children as Storytellers.* Portsmouth, N.H.: Heinemann Educational Books.

> This PETA (Primary English Teaching Association) publication from Australia gives a comprehensive guide for individuals wishing to involve children in storytelling as a means for developing oracy skills and building confidence. Based on prac-

tical experience of working with children as storytellers, this is an easily accessible text with many stimulating and workable ideas. It establishes a rationale for storytelling by children, offers techniques for finding, learning, and presenting stories, and for using stories across the curriculum. Excellent bibliographies of stories for students to tell are included.

————. 1993. Storytelling Links across the Curriculum. *The Literature Base* 4(1):14–17.

This article gives a variety of practical ways to use storytelling across all curriculum areas. Some of the strategies require the use of simple props such as photographs, newspaper headlines, and sandboxes. All the activities have been used successfully in schools from preschool to grade 10.

Nietzke, Doug. 1988. The Ancient New Method. *Clearinghouse* (May):419–21.

This brief article shows how classroom teachers can tell stories of personal experience to improve rapport with their students. Both entertaining and memorable, Nietzke's illustrations of informal storytelling as a learning and community-building tool set an example for us all.

Paley, Vivian Gussin. 1990. *The Boy Who Would Be a Helicopter.* Cambridge, Mass.: Harvard University Press.

Another compelling work by Paley, the outstanding early childhood educator in Chicago. Through classroom observations and anecdotal records, Paley looks at the powerful connections between language development and the development of the story frameworks in young children.

Pellowski, Anne. 1990. *Hidden Stories in Plants: Unusual and Easy-to-Tell Stories from Around the World, Together with Creative Things to Do While Telling Them.* New York: Macmillan Children's Book Group.

The title tells it all. A wonderful enhancement for science curricula!

Rosen, Betty. 1988. *And None of It Was Nonsense: The Power of Storytelling in School.* Portsmouth, N.H.: Heinemann Educational Books.

The story of an inner-city London high school teacher who takes her diverse multicultural group of boy learners from eight to eighteen years of age into the world of ancient myth and legend. They gain courage as writers and tellers and work through their own painful lives through the stories they choose to retell. The kind of book one goes back to again and again.

Sarris, Greg. 1990. Storytelling in the Classroom: Crossing Vexed Chasms. *College English* 52(2):169–85.

Sarris reveals "the potential for storytelling to empower and engage culturally diverse students while providing, in turn, a context for strong critical thinking for students and teachers alike." Sarris's stories about students in his classroom, his own Native American childhood, and the extracurricular lives of his students demonstrate how students see the classroom text through the screen of their own stories. By encouraging this critical skill, Sarris argues, teachers can help students take responsibility for their own learning and feel that the classroom is their own.

Schwartz, Marni. 1985. Finding Myself in My Stories. *Language Arts* 62(7):725–29.

———. 1987. Connecting to Language through Story. *Language Arts* 64(6):603–10.

These two articles help teachers know why and how to share storytelling with students. In the first, Schwartz tells how she came to discover storytelling and in the second how she gets children to search their story pasts for tales to tell and to think of stories as gifts to share rather than as performances.

———. 1990. Storytelling in High School? Naturally. In *Vital Signs 1: Bringing Together Reading and Writing*, edited by James Collins. Portsmouth, N.H.: Boynton Cook.

In this article, Schwartz encourages teachers of older students to see the value of storytelling to bring literature and a study of individual authors and of history alive.

Sierra, Judy, and Robert Kamiski. 1991. *Multicultural Folktales: Stories to Tell Young Children*. Phoenix, Ariz.: Oryx Press.

See annotation under "The Art of Storytelling."

Watts, Irene N. 1992. *Making Stories*. Portsmouth, N.H.: Heinemann Educational Books.

Watts is a Canadian author-playwright and storyteller who gives excellent suggestions in this publication for getting students to develop their own stories. Her ideas give structure to the task of telling a story about something that really happened to you. The focus of the book is unusual ways to get started in story making by using readily available materials as teachers learn how to work with students. Included are suggestions for teaching students how to find stories in the news, how to use letters as stories, and how to uncover stories through updating folktales.

Favorite Story Collections

Barchers, Suzanne I. 1990. *Wise Women: Folk and Fairy Tales from Around the World*. Englewood, Colo.: Libraries Unlimited.

A collection of traditional tales featuring female protagonists who are wise and resourceful rather than weak and passive, thus offering alternatives to stereotypical female and male gender roles.

Baylor, Byrd. 1987. *And It Is Still That Way*. Santa Fe, N.M.: Trails West Publishing.

Arizona Indian "pourquoi" tales that explain natural phenomena. Excellent creative writing models for older children.

Brody, Ed, Jay Goldspinner, Katie Green, Rona Leventhal, and John Porocino, eds. 1992. *Spinning Tales, Weaving Hope: Stories, Storytelling and Activities for Peace, Justice, and the Environment*. Philadelphia: New Society Publishers.

Written for teachers or youth leaders, this book is a collection of stories that transmit values of acceptance of self and others, environmental awareness, and peace. Each story comes with exercises that extend the story into play and discussion. Included are an age-suitability index, a thematic index, and an extensive bibliography for tales on the book's themes.

Bruchac, Joseph. 1985. *Iroquois Stories: Heroes and Heroines, Monsters and Magic*. Freedom, Calif.: Crossing Press.

With great love and respect, Bruchac passes on stories he has been given permission to tell by the Iroquois people. An Abenacki himself, Bruchac seems to have dedicated his life to preserving stories and helping others to understand the sacred tradition from which these stories come. The introduction is a wonderful invitation to the reader to go beyond the stories to more learning about native peoples.

————. 1989. *Return of the Sun: Native American Tales from the Northeast Woodlands*. Freedom, Calif.: Crossing Press.

"Stories are the life of a people. They tell of the deepest hopes and fears of a nation," Bruchac writes in his introduction. Again, as in *Iroquois Stories*, this respectful collector helps us see the context from which these stories come, and he credits the tellers who have shared their tales.

Cathon, Laura E., Marion C. Haushalter, and Virginia A. Russell, eds. 1974. *Stories to Tell Children: A Selected List*. 8th ed. Pittsburgh: University of Pittsburgh Press.

Lists of stories are grouped according to age and interest level. Topics are varied, and several stories are suggested under each topical area.

Chase, Richard. 1943. *Jack Tales*. Boston: Houghton Mifflin.

Collected and retold by Chase, these tales have been handed

down for generations in the North Carolina and Virginia mountains. Told in regional dialect, the tales are suitable for all ages. A favorite resource for tellers.

————. 1948. *Grandfather Tales.* Boston: Houghton Mifflin. More tales from the Appalachians. Many are variants of familiar tales.

Colwell, Eileen. 1977. *A Storyteller's Choice: A Selection of Stories.* London: Bodley Head.

One in a series of storytelling anthologies by this author. Full-text stories are included. A special index in each book gives age and interest level, telling time, and telling suggestions for each story. The teller is advised where the story may be cut to shorten the telling time.

Corrin, Sara, and Steven Corrin, eds. 1974. *Stories for Under-Fives.* Winchester, Mass.: Faber and Faber.

See next entry.

Corrin, Sara. 1989. *Stories for Five-Year-Olds.* Winchester, Mass.: Faber and Faber.

These books contain an excellent collection of full-text stories for preschoolers. The introductory section provides analysis of the literature needs of young children that will aid in selecting other appropriate stories.

Courlander, Harold. 1957. *The Hat-Shaking Dance and Other Ashanti Tales from Ghana.* New York: Harcourt, Brace and World.

This is a collection of stories about Anansi, the trickster hero of the Ashanti people of Ghana. The tales provide explanations for everything, from why all stories belong to Anansi to why spiders' heads are bald and they live in the grass. Variants of these stories can also be found throughout the Caribbean, and vestiges of Anansi appear in the antics of Br'er Rabbit in the United States.

DeVos, Gail. 1991. *Storytelling for Young Adults: Techniques and Treasury.* Englewood, Colo.: Libraries Unlimited.

An excellent anthology of stories that can be told in middle and high school classrooms. The collection is indexed by subject matter as well as by author and includes an excellent bibliography. The stories represent a diverse cultural selection, both contemporary and ancient.

Erdoes, Richard, and Alfonso Ortiz, eds. 1984. *American Indian Myths and Legends.* New York: Pantheon Books.

This collection of Native American myths and legends is an excellent resource for anyone who wants to explore this frequently misunderstood genre. Stories are grouped according to types: stories of world creation, tales of the moon and stars, monsters and monster slayers, ghosts and the spirit world are a few examples. Each section begins with an introduction which provides the reader with helpful information concerning the cultural and historical contexts within which the stories function. Especially important for Native American tales, each story is identified as to the tribe and teller from which it was collected and, in most cases, the date of collection. This is in contrast to many collections which give no tribal affiliation and no recognition to the storyteller. (Please note: these tales have not been selected specifically for children, especially the section entitled "Tales of Love and Lust"!) This collection may best be viewed as a reference and resource book, rather than a book one would freely and directly use with students.

Fairman, Tony (reteller). 1993. *Bury My Bones but Keep My Words: African Tales for Retelling.* New York: Henry Holt.

Fairman includes descriptions of the people and places in Africa where these tales are still being told. He includes a pronunciation guide and music for some of the tales.

Hamilton, Virginia. 1985. *The People Could Fly: The Book of Black Folktales.* New York: Alfred A. Knopf.

These twenty-four selections are retold African American folktales of animals, fantasy, the supernatural, and the desire for freedom. A solid collection of African American folklore exquisitely illustrated by Leo and Dianne Dillon. A Caldecott Medal winner.

Haviland, Virginia, ed. 1979. *North American Legends.* New York: Collins.

An excellent collection of legends from different sectors of the North American continent. Eskimo, Native American, African American, European immigrant, and American tall tales are included.

Iarusso, Marilyn Berg. 1977. *Stories: A List of Stories to Tell and to Read Aloud.* 7th ed. New York: New York Public Library.

Annotated lists of stories that are categorized for telling or reading aloud. Appendixes categorize stories by country of origin and topic/theme.

Leach, Maria. 1974. *Whistle in the Graveyard: Folktales to Chill Your Bones.* New York: Viking Press.

Those ghost stories middle-grade children love to hear are found in this collection. Short, easy-to-learn, easy-to-read stories are included for children to read and tell themselves.

Lester, Julius. 1969. *Black Folktales*. New York: Grove Press.

> Lester uses the vernacular of the late 1960s to retell a variety of African and African American folktales. The collection demonstrates the evolution and continuity of African American storytelling style.

———. 1987. *The Tales of Uncle Remus: The Adventures of Brer Rabbit*. New York: Dial Press.

> Frustrated by the dialect in the Joel Chandler Harris collections, Lester undertook to retell the old stories in a more contemporary vernacular. A fresh look at some old favorites. In 1988, Lester published a second collection, *More Tales of Uncle Remus: Further Adventures of Brer Rabbit, His Friends, Enemies, and Others*.

Lurie, Alison, ed. 1980. *Clever Gretchen and Other Forgotten Folktales*. New York: HarperCollins Children's Books.

> A collection of nonsexist fairy tales with female protagonists who fight and hunt as well as any man, defeat giants, answer riddles, outwit the devil, and rescue their friends and relatives from all sorts of danger and evil spells.

MacDonald, Margaret Read. 1986. *Twenty Tellable Tales*. Bronx, N.Y.: H. W. Wilson.

> Both new and experienced storytellers will find some gold to mine in this book! It contains twenty folktales from around the world which invite listeners actively to participate. Following each story are notes to better equip the tellers. Some include a melody for a line or phrase; others suggest gestures and movement. Background information on the stories is also provided. An unusual and helpful feature is the printing of each folktale in ethnopoetic format, structuring phrases or sentences like a poem for ease of learning. A second section provides information on finding, learning, and telling stories. The book concludes with a third, shorter section containing a list of story sources.

Miller, Theresa, Anne Pellowski, and Norma Livo, eds. 1988. *Joining In: An Anthology of Audience Participation Stories and How to Tell Them*. Cambridge, Mass.: Yellow Moon Press.

> An excellent source for tellers who want to involve their audience in the telling of a story. Stories suggested by well-known storytellers.

Minard, Rosemary, ed. 1975. *Womenfolk and Fairy Tales*. Boston: Houghton Mifflin.

> An early collection of "feminist" fairy tales featuring heroines who are "active, intelligent, capable, and courageous." The tales reflect a variety of cultures—Celtic, European, Scandinavian, Japanese, Chinese, Persian, and African.

Morgan, Sally. 1993. *The Flying Emu and Other Australian Stories.* New York: Alfred A. Knopf.

This collection of stories by internationally known aboriginal artist and writer Sally Morgan conveys the spirit and humor of traditional aboriginal tales. These stories were inspired by the many oral tales told to the author when she was a child by her mother and grandmother. All the stories are written with the clear voice of the storyteller and are eminently suitable for oral sharing. Morgan's stunning illustrations, with their vibrant colors and rich patterns, perfectly complement these tales.

National Association for the Preservation and Perpetuation of Storytelling. 1991. *Best-Loved Stories at the National Storytelling Festival.* Jonesborough, Tenn.: National Storytelling Press.

This is a twentieth anniversary collection of thirty-seven traditional and adapted folk and fairy tales, original tales, true narratives, and ghost stories told at the annual National Storytelling Festival from 1973 to 1990. Included is information about the storytellers, the tales, and the background of the festival, which is sponsored by the National Association for the Preservation and Perpetuation of Storytelling. Followed in 1992 by *More Best-Loved Stories Told at the National Storytelling Festival.*

Papineau, Andre. 1989. *Jesus on the Mend: Healing Stories for Ordinary People.* San Jose, Calif.: Resource Publications.

This is a book of stories about people, of something that went wrong in their lives, and how they fixed it or came to terms with it. The reflection following each story, rather than explaining "what the story means," invites the reader or teller into a mental dialogue with the writer. Useful in religious and nonreligious settings.

Parks, Van Dyke, and Malcolm Jones. 1986. *Jump! The Adventures of Brer Rabbit by Joel Chandler Harris.* San Diego, Calif.: Harcourt Brace Jovanovich.

Parks and his collaborators have adapted Joel Chandler Harris's retellings of the Br'er Rabbit stories in a vernacular that is more comfortable to contemporary ears. Contains five tellable tales with beautiful illustrations by Barry Moser, and concludes with a song from the record "JUMP!" by Van Dyke Parks. Other books in the series are *Jump Again!* (1987) and *Jump on Over!* (1989).

Pellowski, Anne. 1984. *The Story Vine: A Source Book of Unusual and Easy-to-Tell Stories from Around the World.* New York: Macmillan Children's Book Group.

A delightful anthology of stories told with string, pictures, sand, dolls, and finger play, as well as stories that feature drawing, riddling, and musical instruments.

Phelps, Ethel Johnston, ed. 1978. *Tatterhood and Other Tales.* New York: Feminist Press.

————. 1981. *The Maid of the North: Feminist Folk Tales from Around the World.* New York: Holt, Rinehart & Winston.

Both collections contain tales whose female protagonists are strong, resourceful, and wise. Notes at the end of each book give the source of each tale and some background information. Excellent tales for telling!

Sagel, Jim. 1988. *Sabelotodo Entiendelonada and Other Stories.* Tempe, Ariz.: Bilingual Press/Editorial Bilingue.

This is a collection of six stories told in English and a regional dialect of Spanish. The delightful stories are filled with humor and poignancy, set in the multicultural environment of the northern New Mexico highlands.

Sauvageau-Pro, Juan. 1989. *Stories that Must Not Die.* Los Angeles: Pan American Publishing Co.

An extensive collection of folktales and legends of Mexico and the southwest states. Written both in English and Spanish, the stories range from stories about animals, to unusual heroes, to ghosts.

Schram, Peninnah, and Steven M. Rosman. 1992. *Eight Tales for Eight Nights: Stories for Chanukah.* Northvale, N.J.: Jason Aronson.

In their introduction, Schram and Rosman say that their "How Chanukah Came to Be" is meant to act as a shammash, kindling each of the next eight tales, which explore a wealth of themes such as freedom, thanksgiving, dedication, the miracle of lights, Jewish heroes and heroines, Jewish pride, and miracles. This book would be wonderful to share over the "eight nights" or at any other time of year.

Schwartz, Alvin. 1986. *Scary Stories to Tell in the Dark.* New York: Harper and Row.

Short, easy-to-learn stories, many with a humorous twist. Schwartz has included "eerie" tales as well as some clever "jump stories." Companion books to expand your repertoire of spooky stories are his *More Scary Stories to Tell in the Dark* (1987) and *Scary Stories 3: More Tales to Chill Your Bones* (1991).

Sierra, Judy, and Robert Kaminski. 1991. *Multicultural Folktales: Stories to Tell Young Children.* Phoenix, Ariz.: Oryx Press.

See annotation in "Art of Storytelling" section.

Singer, Isaac Bashevis. 1968. *When Schlemiel Went to Warsaw and Other Stories.* New York: Farrar, Strauss, and Giroux.

A delightful and personal rendering of Yiddish folktales told to Singer by his mother and grandmother. In the best tradition of storytelling, Singer retells the tales in his own style, re-creating and personalizing them, yet retaining the flavor of the original stories, even to the detail of mentioning the same towns and villages he heard in the stories as a child. Your audiences will be driven into fits of laughter as they hear the title story and other stories in this fine collection.

Tashjian, Virginia A. 1969. *Juba This and Juba That.* Boston: Little, Brown.

————. 1974. *With a Deep Sea Smile: Story Hour Sketches for Large or Small Groups.* Boston: Little, Brown.

In addition to some clever, amusing stories, Tashjian has included story hour "stretchers" in these "must-have" books. Songs, fingerplays, action songs, riddles, tongue twisters, and jokes are provided which are quite useful to "get the wiggles out" of young listeners before you begin your new story.

Yolen, Jane, ed. 1986. *Favorite Folktales from Around the World.* New York: Pantheon Books.

A treasure of a folktale collection, edited by an accomplished storyteller. The anthology is categorized by such headings as "Tricksters, Rogues, and Cheats" and "Fools: Numskulls and Noodleheads." Each of the thirteen subject categories has ten or more stories from identified countries around the world, with notes explaining the source for each tale and providing some background information. The introduction is a thoughtful essay on the power and use of stories. An excellent resource for educators or storytellers looking for tales from the Australian Aborigines to Iceland. The sections of biographical notes and the acknowledgments lead the reader even further in the search for the perfect tale.

Sourcebooks

MacDonald, Margaret Read. 1982. *The Storyteller's Sourcebook: A Subject, Title, and Motif Index to Folklore Collections for Children.* Detroit: Gale Research.

This comprehensive source for finding stories is cross-referenced by subject, title, and motif.

Polette, Nancy, and Marjorie Hamlin. 1977. *Celebrating with Books.* Metuchen, N.J.: Scarecrow Press.

This sourcebook contains annotated bibliographies of stories related to special seasons and holidays.

Other Resources

The National Association for the Preservation and Perpetuation of Storytelling, located in Jonesborough, Tennessee, is the national association for storytellers in the United States. It is a nonprofit organization "dedicated to encouraging the practice and application of the storytelling art." It provides many services for storytellers, including sponsoring the National Storytelling Festival every year on the first weekend in October; publishing two journals for storytellers, *Yarnspinner* and *The Storytelling Magazine;* and maintaining an excellent catalogue of resources for storytellers. Address: P.O. Box 309, Jonesborough, TN 37659. Telephone: (615)753-2171.

Theoretical Perspectives

Bauman, Richard. 1975. Verbal Art as Performance. *American Anthropologist* 77:290–311.

> The first of many articles and books by a folklorist who has studied and theorized folk performance. Bauman observes here that narrative performances (stories told) require a relationship between the storyteller (performer), an informed audience, and the frames of the stories themselves as they are understood inside the culture.

———. 1978. *Verbal Art as Performance.* Rowley, Mass.: Newbury House Publishers.

> Written from the perspective of folklore and linguistic anthropology, Bauman's book departs from a conception of verbal art that is text centered, to an exploration of verbal art as performance, as a particular "species of situated human communication." He discusses the interpretive frame which verbal performance sets up and its "assumption of responsibility to an audience for a display of communicative competence." Supplementary essays, three dealing with verbal art in particular cultures, make up the second portion of the book.

Bausch, William J. 1984. *Storytelling, Imagination and Faith.* Mystic, Conn.: Twenty-Third Publications.

> This is a book intended for religious educators but helpful to all storytellers. Bausch, a member of the clergy who tells stories, tells many of his favorites as he explores the importance of stories to our humanity and our understanding of one another. The chapter on the characteristics of story is especially fine. He puts story into a framework that is helpful in first learning to tell.

Bruner, Jerome. 1986. *Actual Minds, Possible Worlds.* Cambridge, Mass.: Harvard University Press.

A thoughtful discussion of Bruner's insights into narrative thought. He compares narrative thought to paradigmatic thought, describing both as primary ways of thinking for human beings.

―――. 1990. *Acts of Meaning.* Cambridge, Mass.: Harvard University Press.

In this book, Bruner discusses human narrative and develops a theory of "folk psychology." In his words, the central theme of the book is "the nature and cultural shaping of meaning-making and the central place it plays in human action" (xii). Bruner describes and gives examples of how it is through stories that human beings of all ages shape meaning in their lives.

Dundes, Alan. 1965. *The Study of Folklore.* Englewood Cliffs, N.J.: Prentice-Hall.

An outstanding anthology of scholarly articles on folklore and storytelling. The collection provides important background about the origins of folklore.

Egan, Kieran. 1989. *Teaching as Storytelling: An Alternative Approach to Teaching and Curriculum in the Elementary School.* Chicago: University of Chicago Press.

Egan lays out a convincing argument for the power of story and storytelling as a teaching tool in the restructured elementary school program. Using a historical viewpoint, he notes the use of story as an effective teaching model in past civilizations and suggests a modern curriculum that harnesses the power of story and students' natural curiosity and imagination as learning evolves.

Ong, Walter J. 1982. *Orality and Literacy: The Technologizing of the Word.* New York: Routledge, Chapman, & Hall.

Ong explores the differences between oral and literate cultures and the thought processes that accompany reading as opposed to listening and speaking.

Propp, Vladimir. 1968. *Morphology of the Folktale,* translated by Laurence Scott. Austin: University of Texas Press. (Originally published in Leningrad in 1928)

A classic study of the structural patterns in Russian folktales, which laid the foundations for research on story grammar. The book offers insights into the structures of oral storytelling as well.

Rosen, Harold. 1986. The Importance of Story. *Language Arts* 63(3):226–37.

Rosen explores the nature of narrative and its primary function in human experience. He points out the importance of the narrator and draws a distinction between a mere "reciter" and a "reteller" or "animator" of a story. He discusses the abuses of narrative in education, most specifically the "reductiveness and schematism which pick away at narrative until we are left with the bare bones." Rosen calls for the replacing of "authoritative discourse" in the curriculum with the "internally persuasive discourse" of narrative. There's a lot of meat in this brief but important article!

————. 1992. The Power of Story. *Teachers Networking: The Whole Language Newsletter* 11:1.

Originally a chapter in *Questions and Answers about Whole Language,* a collaboration of Richard C. Owen Publishers, Whole Language Consultants, Ltd., and the Whole Language Umbrella. In this thought-provoking article, Rosen, who has studied narrative extensively, describes the complex activity that storytelling is and how allowing children to practice it is valuable exercise for their minds.

Smardo, Frances A., and John F. Curry. 1982. *What Research Tells Us about Storyhours and Receptive Language.* Dallas: Dallas Public Library.

A research study which compares the benefits of "live" storytelling, video stories, and story films. In addition to supporting the use of "live" storytelling over the other means of presenting stories, the research report includes a comprehensive review of the literature dealing with storytelling.

Stone, Elizabeth. 1988. *Black Sheep and Kissing Cousins: How Our Family Stories Shape Us.* New York: Penguin.

A book about the stories that families tell and pass on to the young, providing insights into the power of stories in our lives. The book discusses and provides examples of stories about family origins, ground rules, definitions, monuments, myths, pecking order, and legacies.

Stone, Kay. 1986. Oral Narration in Contemporary North America. In *Fairy Tales and Society: Illusion, Allusion, and Paradigm,* edited by Ruth B. Bottigheimer. Philadelphia: University of Pennsylvania Press.

Folklore scholar Kay Stone analyzes three kinds of storytelling found in contemporary North America: the "traditional oral narration" found in predominantly rural communities; "nontraditional urban storytelling" found in schools, libraries, and churches; and the "neo-traditional tale-telling" of professional tellers who travel storytelling festival circuits, perform storytelling concerts, and lead storytelling workshops. Stone provides important critical analysis and insight into various approaches to the art and nature of oral narration in North America today.

Wells, Gordon. 1985. *The Meaning Makers: Children Learning Language and Using Language to Learn.* Portsmouth, N.H.: Heinemann Educational Books.

An excellent source for those who are seeking research and theoretical evidence to justify the use of storytelling in the early childhood or early elementary curriculum. Wells's study delineates the impact of exposing children to stories upon the development of their language.

Witherell, Carol, and Nell Noddings. 1991. *Stories Lives Tell: Narrative and Dialogue in Teacher Education.* New York: Teachers College Press.

A collection of articles written by teachers and researchers about the power of narrative to shape meaning in our lives, and specifically in education. The editors offer three themes: the role of narrative in teaching and counseling, the primacy of caring and dialogue in educational practice, and narrative and dialogue as a model for teaching and learning.

Yolen, Jane. 1981. *Touch Magic: Fantasy, Faerie and Folklore in the Literature of Childhood.* New York: Philomel.

This book of essays provides a history of folklore and describes why we need stories and need to hear them *told* in order to be able to enter the "land of illusion" as readers. Yolen is an artful storyteller herself, as well as a writer of fantasy and fairy tales. For those who need convincing—and for those who don't!—this is an important book.

References

Arbuthnot, May Hill. 1957. *Children and Books.* Chicago: Scott-Foresman.

Barton, Bob, and David Booth. 1990. *Stories in the Classroom: Storytelling, Reading Aloud and Role-playing with Children.* Portsmouth, N.H.: Heinemann Educational Books.

Bauman, Richard. 1975. Verbal Art as Performance. *American Anthropologist* 77:290–311.

Berger, Peter, and Thomas Luckman. 1977. *The Social Construction of Reality.* New York: Anchor.

Brown, Fred. 1991. Highlands to Hollers. *Storytelling Magazine* 3:14–16.

Bruner, Jerome. 1990. *Acts of Meaning.* Cambridge, Mass.: Harvard University Press.

Caudill, Rebecca. 1965. *A Certain Small Shepherd.* New York: Holt.

Chase, Richard. 1943. *Jack Tales.* Boston: Houghton Mifflin.

Dundes, Alan. 1964. Texture, Text and Context. *Southern Folklore Quarterly* 28:251–65.

Goldstein, Kenneth. 1964. *A Guide for Fieldworkers in Folklore.* Hatboro, Pa.: Folklore Associates.

Hamilton, Martha, and Mitch Weiss. 1960. *Children Tell Stories: A Teaching Guide.* Katonah, N.Y.: Richard C. Owens.

Huck, Charlotte, Susan Helper, and Janet Hickman. 1987. *Children's Literature in the Elementary School.* 4th ed. New York: Holt, Rinehart and Winston.

Lawson, Robert. 1989. *Robbut: A Tale of Tails.* New York: Viking. (Reprint of the original first published in the 1950s)

Mikkelsen, Nina. 1990. Toward Greater Equity in Literacy Education: Story Making and Non-mainstream Students. *Language Arts* 67:556–66.

Oring, Elliott. 1986. On the Concepts of Folklore. In *Folk Groups and Folklore Genres: An Introduction,* edited by Elliott Oring, 71–91. Logan: University of Utah Press.

Parks, Tomas. 1990. Personal communication, December 11.

Rylant, Cynthia. 1985. *The Relatives Came.* New York: Bradbury Press.

Santino, Jack. 1983. Miles of Smiles, Years of Struggle: The Negotiation of Black Occupational Identity through Personal Experience Narrative. *Journal of American Folklore* 96:393–410.

Shimmel, Nancy. 1982. *Just Enough to Make a Story: A Sourcebook for Storytelling.* Berkeley, Calif.: Sister's Choice Press.

Schwartz, Alvin. 1981. *Scary Stories to Tell in the Dark.* New York: Harper and Row.

Editors

Ann M. Trousdale is assistant professor at Louisiana State University, where she teaches courses in children's literature, language arts, and storytelling. She has also taught on the elementary, junior high, and high school levels. She has told stories in schools, churches, and club meetings, as well as at the Swapping Ground at NCTE conferences and at Tellebration!—a nationwide storytelling event sponsored by the National Association for the Preservation and Perpetuation of Storytelling. Her research interests focus on social issues in children's books, on children's responses to literature, particularly to fairy tales, and on storytelling.

Sue Woestehoff is professor of education at the University of Michigan–Flint, where she teaches courses in elementary language arts and children's literature. Her research interests are related to folklore, storytelling, multiculturalism, and children's book illustrations. She has authored, among other things, "Children's Literature in the Classroom" in *The Scott, Foresman Anthology of Children's Literature.* A member of NCTE since the mid-1960s, she has served as chair of the Committee on Storytelling, chair of the Children's Literature Assembly, and as a member of both the Commission on Literature and the Elementary Section Nominating Committee.

Marni Schwartz "discovered" storytelling as a middle school English teacher, when she realized she had been telling and hearing others tell stories since her "tip me over, pour me out" days. Now, as a full-time teller and consultant and as founder of The Story Studio, she works with schools, universities, business and civic groups, museums, libraries, and arts and recreation programs to spread the good word about the potential of storytelling for learning and living. Her articles have appeared in *Language Arts, English Journal, Workshop 2,* and *Vital Signs.* She is currently at work on a book for teachers about the use of storytelling for enhancing self-awareness and building community.

Contributors

Barbara A. Connelly recently retired from the Campbell Union School District in California, where she taught grades K–8. She was a mentor teacher in storytelling for three years while serving on the NCTE Committee on Storytelling. She has conducted storytelling inservice for new teachers and workshops at reading conferences and has "told" at book, author, and renaissance fairs. While doing research with the tinkers in Scotland, she won a second-place award at the Storytelling Competition, Traditional Music and Song Association of Scotland. She received a local county award for her outstanding school program in storytelling.

Brian Conroy is a fifth-grade teacher in the Moreland School District in San Jose, California. For the past eleven years he has served as a theater arts specialist and as a mentor teacher in storytelling, folklore, and mythology. Recently he published *What's the Story?*—a book of storytelling activities for student storytellers. He has performed at the National Storytelling Festival and has been featured teller at several other festivals. He has also made workshop presentations at two universities, at the Bay Area Storytelling Festival, and for school districts throughout California.

Karen P. Durand teaches the second grade in Mt. Pleasant, South Carolina. She has published in the *Experienced Teachers Handbook,* an Impact II publication. Along with the spoken word, many of her stories have been stitched with needle and thread.

Julia Hamilton is an English instructor and the campus coordinator for the Writing Across the Curriculum and Critical Thinking projects at Inver Hills Community College, Inver Grove Heights, Minnesota. She has taught high school English in both public and private schools and has been a language arts consultant (7–12). An amateur storyteller, she specializes in personal experience stories and tales with strong female characters. She has made presentations at NCTE-affiliate and community college conferences on the use of story and metaphor in the classroom.

Sharon Kane is associate professor of elementary education at the State University of New York at Oswego. She teaches courses and has published several articles in the areas of reading and whole language. She has presented at national, state, and regional conferences on literacy issues and often visits elementary schools as a storyteller.

Syd Lieberman has taught high school English for twenty-three years, all but three at Evanston Township High School in Evanston, Illinois, and is also a nationally acclaimed storyteller. He has appeared on television;

at major storytelling festivals across the country, including two featured appearances at the National Festival in Jonesborough, Tennessee; and on American Public Radio's "Good Evening" as a guest storyteller and host. The American Library Association named three of his cassette tapes Notable Children's Recordings, and Parents' Choice presented its highest award for two other tapes.

Barbara Lipke is a professional storyteller and educational consultant. She taught elementary school in Brookline, Massachusetts, for twenty-four years and was Teacher as Storyteller in Brookline. She has been a member of the NCTE Committee on Storytelling since its inception and presents regularly at NCTE. She has published articles on using storytelling across the curriculum in *Science Scope, Yarnspinner,* and other publications.

Kerry Mallan is a lecturer in language and literacy education at Queensland University of Technology, Australia. She has been a primary school teacher and a teacher-librarian and has authored several journal articles, a book chapter, and books related to children's literature, storytelling, and teacher-librarianship. Her most recent books are *Children as Storytellers* and *Laugh Lines: Exploring Humour in Children's Literature.* She is currently developing Project SARA (Storytelling And Rural Areas) with the Longreach School of Distance Education, Queensland. The program is devoted to meeting the oracy and literacy needs of children in isolated areas through storytelling.

Ruth Merrill is a "gypo" educator doing private consulting and storytelling in the mountains of Idaho. A former teacher of all ages and a librarian, she now spends her summers atop a Forest Service lookout, reading and writing. She spends the rest of the year developing curriculum and workshops that incorporate storytelling, drama, and literature; volunteering in schools and libraries; and performing in community theater. She collaborated with her husband, John Thomsen, on "Portrait of a Dirty Little Book," a book review for *The Journal of Educational Issues of Language Minority Students.*

Mary Murphy has been telling stories professionally for more than a decade. She has performed or given workshops at the National Storytelling Festival, the Hawaii Storytellers Association Festival, the Clever Gretchen Folklore Conference at Syracuse University, the New York State Imagination Celebration, and the University of Rochester Storytelling Conference. She has recorded an audiotape called *murphy stew.* A resident of Albany, New York, she is a member of the National Association for the Preservation and Perpetuation of Storytelling and is the coordinator of New York State's Mini-Imagination Celebration.

Tom Romano is assistant professor of English at Utah State University, where he teaches courses in creative writing and English education. Before coming to USU, he taught high school for seventeen years in Ohio; his book, *Clearing the Way: Working with Teenage Writers,* is based on that experience. He has also written articles, poems, and book chapters, including "Evolving Voice," published in *Teacher as Writer* (NCTE). In 1992 he served as chair of the nominating committee for the Conference on English Education.

Jeanne Smith is director of composition at Oglala Lakota College, located on the Pine Ridge Reservation in South Dakota, where she has taught for eighteen years. For eight of those years she served as chair of the General Studies Department. She has a strong interest in storytelling, archival research, and oral history and recently completed an extensive archival project, as well as a book of oral histories about early reservation schools. For the next three summers she will direct a Health Careers Opportunity program at the college, using a whole-language approach to the teaching of science. She is currently coordinating the Writing Across the Curriculum project at Oglala Lakota College.

Bonnie S. Sunstein is assistant professor of English education at the University of Iowa in Iowa City. For twenty-five years she taught in secondary schools and colleges in New England, and she continues to serve on the staff of the New Hampshire Summer Writing program. Her interest in folklore studies began while she was a graduate student and continued in the department of anthropology at the University of Wisconsin. She is author of *Summer Revisions* and co-editor, with Donald Graves, of *Portfolio Portraits* and has written numerous articles, book reviews, poems, and chapters in collections. She was president of the National Writing Centers Association and is currently chair of the nominating committee for the Conference on English Education.

Anne Vilen teaches composition and creative writing to college students and adult learners in Denver, Colorado. She has also taught at the Duke Young Writers Camp, a creative-writing camp for grades 6 through 12. Her recent publications include "Stories and Mores: A Blueprint for Moral Education" in *Teaching and Learning: The Journal of Natural Inquiry* and "Forgiveness: A Fishstory" in *New Moon,* a publication for teenage girls.

Joe Yukish is professor of education at Clemson University, where he is also Reading Recovery teacher-leader-trainer at the Southern Regional Reading Recovery Training Center, a program for first-grade children at risk of reading failure. After ten years as an elementary and special education teacher, he trained elementary teachers in reading education, children's literature, and special education. He has provided inservice education for public school personnel and has conducted parent workshops on developing literacy environments for children in the home. As a professional storyteller, he tells stories in public schools and libraries. His publications include *Fishing, My Doll,* and *I Can't Wait to Read.*